Marianne Fischer with Gayle Roper

Time of STORM

The harrowing true story of a Jewish Christian woman in wartime Hungary.

CHRISTIAN HERALD BOOKS
Chappaqua, New York

Library of Congress Cataloging in Publication Data

Fischer, Marianne, 1924 –
   Time of storm.

      1. Holocaust, Jewish (1939– 1945) — Hungary — Budapest —
Personal narratives.   2. Jews — Hungary — Budapest —
Biography.   3. Fischer, Marianne, 1924–
4. Converts from Judaism — Biography.   5. Budapest
(Hungary) — Ethnic relations.   I. Roper, Gayle G.
II. Title.
DS135.H93F574   943.9′052′0924   [B]   80-69310
ISBN 0-915684-82-9   AACR2

Christian Herald, independent, evangelical and interdenominational, is dedicated to publishing wholesome, inspirational and religious books for Christian families.

First Edition
CHRISTIAN HERALD BOOKS, 40 Overlook Drive, Chappaqua,
New York 10514
Printed in the United States of America

for
GEORGE
my constant and loving companion
for
John, Andrea, Robert, and Sylvia
who always arrived when I needed them most
and for
Mary Hajos and Hector and Olive Sinzheimer
my dear friends in the Messiah.

We wish to express special thanks to Andrea Fischer Musser for her generous spirit and for the hours she spent researching, interviewing, and organizing this project.

Contents

1

March!

"*Achtung! Achtung!* Everyone report to the main door immediately! *Mach schnell!*"

At this order, fear spread like wildfire through our ghetto house. There was going to be another march.

Out our window I could see people from the neighboring houses being lined up by twos and pushed along. German soldiers and Hungarian guards stalked about, the midday sun glancing off their weapons.

Mama, Papa, and I had just sat down with some of the other occupants of our apartment for our noon meal. My body, swollen with the new life growing in it, yearned to finish my small portion of soup, but I dared not.

I grabbed my warm coat and the small straw bag I had packed in anticipation of such a marching order. Those about me were stuffing small necessities into their pockets — toothbrushes, cigarettes, and changes of underwear. I took one last spoonful of soup and hurriedly followed Mama and Papa out the door.

Hundreds of people from our block were being formed into a long line. Friends, neighbors, and strangers, all wore the same anxious expression. Children whimpered in fear at still another disruption of their already unstable lives. Old people looked for strong, young arms to lean on. Everywhere the yellow Star of

David bloomed on chests, the visible evidence of the stigma of being a Jew in Budapest, Hungary, in October, 1944.

A whisper passed down the line, "They're taking rings."

I looked at the shiny new band on my left hand. It was enough they had taken George; they were not going to take his ring. I ripped a hole in the lining of my coat and dropped the ring in.

"All jewelry," ordered a guard, close now, holding out the bag to Papa.

Reluctantly, Papa slipped his wedding band off his finger. How many times as a child had I tried to slip that ring over my wrist, so big it seemed? Now he dropped it into the sack to be lost forever. Mama dropped hers in, too.

The guard stopped in front of me. I held out my empty hands and silently showed him that I wore no ring. He passed on.

I rejoiced in my small victory.

The line of people began to move forward. In front of us a few paces, old Mr. Haz lost his balance in the press of the crowd and fell.

"Stop! He's fallen," cried a woman near him. As she bent to help him, a rifle butt prodded her sharply, throwing her off balance.

"Keep moving!"

The woman, anguish on her face, was pushed ahead by the hundreds of people behind her.

"Papa, Mr. Haz! He'll be trampled!"

"Keep moving," shouted the soldiers, forcing us forward.

My heart ached. It terrified me that the guards were so callous about the old man's fate. Papa, who always understood, patted my shoulder gently. We marched on and I held my coat close against the cold and the fear.

I thought of George. Where was he? Was he still alive? If I were actually on my way to be killed, would he ever find out what happened to me?

A phrase echoed through my mind. "Though I walk through the valley of the shadow of death, I will fear no evil. . . Thou art with me. . . Thou art with me."

The fear drained away and an unexplicable calm settled over me. It was real then, this new relationship I had with God.

We marched for over an hour. All about me faces reflected fear; beneath the fear some showed determination, while others held only a haunted helplessness. To them the uncertainty about life and the constant terror of unknown death were beyond bearing. Only weeks before in our neatly kept ghetto courtyard, a scream and a thud chillingly told of one woman's desperation. She had chosen sure swift death over uncertain life, and had leapt from her fifth floor window. Who could blame her?

I glanced at Papa and saw his face pinched with chill and fear. Mama clutched at my arm. Cold and fatigue nipped at my heels, and like a pair of vicious dogs sought to pull me down. I resisted, focusing all my energy on the process of putting one foot before the other. Those near me in the line pulled their worn and inadequate garments about them as if hoping that by warming their bodies they could also warm their spirits.

After an endless walk, we reached our destination, a large racetrack outside Budapest, its great oval dominating the landscape, its gates swallowing those who walked before me with fearful efficiency.

By the time I walked through the arched entrance, perhaps a thousand shivering, anxious people huddled in grim silence on the grassy ring. I looked beyond them and immediately saw the reason for their unnatural quiet.

In the bleachers surrounding the racetrack were soldiers, and beside each was a machine gun mounted on a tripod. Each gun was pointed at us.

I looked at Papa, and he put his arm reassuringly about me. Mama leaned in the protective circle of his other arm. We stood together, waiting to die.

Nothing happened.

Rumors began. "In an hour. . . just waiting for dark. . . need the final order."

I was tired, I was hungry, and I ached. I saw some of the older people sitting on the ground, and I sat, too.

"Mari, it's too cold for you to sit down, too damp," said Papa. "It's not good for the child you carry."

"I'm sorry, Papa, I'm just too tired."

"If only I could get to the stables," he said. "I could get you some hay to sit on. There must be some left."

"You mustn't even think of trying, Papa." I looked at the guards, their bayonets spitting sunlight. "I'll be fine."

Suddenly a voice spoke nearby. "Dezsö Komlos, is that you?"

Papa turned to answer, and we saw a man in the uniform of the Hungarian Civil Police.

"Imre Szabo," said Papa. "After all these years. You look well."

"Turn away when you speak to me, Dezsö. I can't be seen talking to a Jew. I feel sorry for you, but I don't want to make trouble for myself."

"Just one small favor then, Imre. My daughter is nearly five months pregnant, and she shouldn't be sitting on the damp ground. There must be hay left in the stables. Just an armful would be enough."

The guard walked away without answering.

"Who is he, Papa?"

"An old friend from the First War. We fought side by side then. Now Hitler's poison has made us like strangers." He sighed. Hate was a difficult emotion for Papa to comprehend.

There was movement in the bleachers. I forgot all about the hay as the soldiers began readying their machine guns. What would I do when they began firing? I couldn't run; there was no place to go. I could play dead, but for how long? Surely the guards would check for survivors and find me and kill me, probably with a bayonet. I shuddered. A bullet would be better.

I thought of George again and reached into my straw bag for a picture I had there. I looked at the little photo of myself and remembered the day George had taken it. We had developed it together, and it had become his favorite of me. As I looked at it, I felt certain that George was still alive. If only there were some way of letting him know what had happened to me.

"Look! Imre's coming back." Papa was clearly surprised.

Walking toward us but not acknowledging us was the guard, Imre Szabo. He was carrying half a bale of hay. As he walked by us, eyes averted, he carefully let a few sections of the hay fall to the ground.

"Please, sir," I called to him. He flinched. He'd been so careful not to appear involved with us. "Take this." I thrust the picture of myself into his hand. "After the war, if you can find George Fischer, tell him where I was at the end."

Szabo hesitated, his face a reflection of warring emotions. Pity for me finally won over his fear, and he took the picture and disappeared into the crowd. I felt gratitude for the risk he took for me.

We spread the hay on the ground, sat back to back for support, and waited. The sun and my overwhelming tiredness made me relax. I slept.

I had been born twenty years before on April 29, 1924, on Papa's birthday. I was the fourth Komlos child, the second and only surviving daughter. Whether it was my only daughter status or our mutual birthdays, I'm not certain, but I think Papa was always partial to me.

Tall, powerfully built, but gentle and loving, my Papa was wonderful. He ran his butcher's business with style and joy. He worked hard for six days out of every week, and he loved to relax after work with a game of cards.

"It's all right," said Mama of Papa's stops at the coffee house every day after work for cards. "After all, some men chase women."

Papa was proud to be a Jew. Each morning when he arose, he strapped the phylacteries to his forehead and arms, faced Jerusalem and prayed. At holiday temple services, he carried the Torah, a sign of honor. At these times of religious ritual, a look of joy would cover his face.

Mama was short with a pouter pigeon bosom. We called her our "dumpling." She was also a devout Jew. She had a prayerbook that Papa had given her early in their marriage, and she read from it every night before she went to sleep. She faithfully attended Sabbath services and saw to the lighting of the Sabbath candles. She taught me to be proud of my heritage.

Papa's Judaism, though deeply felt, was somewhat expedient. He ate pork and broke minor laws if breaking them was more convenient than keeping them. Not so Mama. She kept herself and the house kosher and firmly believed all the laws were equally important.

Passover was especially exciting to me each year. When we sat down to the Seder feast, Papa would read from the Haggadah, and the ancient story of the Hebrews' flight from Egypt would come alive. But it was I, as the youngest around our table, who began the celebration by asking the age-old question, "What makes this day different from another day?" For once I was more important than my brothers, Alex and Jules.

Alex was seven years older than I, a tease and great

fun. Jules was three years my senior and far more serious and studious than either Alex or I. Papa expected great things from his sons, but it was Mama who saw to it that they performed as expected.

When I was two-and-a-half and Jules was five-and-a-half, Fraulein Anna came to live with us. She was our governess while Mama helped Papa in the butcher shop.

Often Fraulein Anna would take us from our two-bedroom apartment on Elemer Utca to the butcher shop on Nefelets Utca 41. There Papa, tall and handsome in his long white apron, would lift me in his arms and show me off to his customers. Then would come my favorite time. Papa would take me to the smokehouse behind the shop and give me a piece of freshly smoked meat to nibble.

Surprisingly, Christmas was an exciting time for me. Fraulein Anna (Frauli) was not Jewish, but because Mama and Papa thought so much of her, they let her have a Christmas tree in our apartment. I would help her decorate it with candles, sparklers, and colorfully wrapped candies. When the carolers came — children dressed as shepherds and singing about angels — Frauli would let me throw them pennies.

"Remember, Mari," Papa would caution. "This is not our holiday. It is fun, yes, but we have Chanukah. We light our candles and we have the dreidel to play with. We are Jews."

When I was five, I contracted scarlet fever. For six weeks I hovered between life and death. Mama and Papa wouldn't let me go the hospital because it was there that their first daughter Ilonka had died of the same disease at the age of two. Instead Mama was my nurse, staying with me constantly.

During my illness I asked Mama to tell me one story over and over. An orphan boy inherited a violin. Though he was very poor, he would not sell it. One day he was playing it, and it slipped from his hands and fell to the ground. It broke, revealing a fortune inside. The concept that good could come from the least expected sources became part of my personal philosophy.

When I recovered from the scarlet fever, I was left with a weakened heart.

"Move to the suburbs," the doctors said. "It will be better for her."

So we moved to Kispest, a suburb of Budapest, to Eotvos Utca 26. We lived there four years while I attended the Jewish elementary school, a fifteen-minute walk from my home. I always liked school though I never did as well as Jules.

When it was time to enter the *gymnasium* or secondary school, my heart had improved and we moved back to Budapest.

In the summer my cousins would often come to see us, and Klara, my favorite cousin, would stay for long visits. We were a loving, close-knit family. I knew I was fortunate.

I also knew I was different. I didn't have to go far to see a placard on a fence reading *Büdös Zsidó!* "Dirty Jew." Often as we walked to school, Gentile children would taunt us, *"Büdös Zsidó! Dirty Jew!"*

"Büdös Zsidó!" The epithet was loud and cutting. I snapped back from my memories and remembered where I was. The sky above the racetrack was darkening into night, and the air was growing chill. I shifted uncomfortably. Again the coarse, cruel voice yelled out, *"Büdös Zsidó!"*

I wondered what the crude guard would say if I told him I was a Christian now, that I acknowledged Jesus as the Messiah.

"Impossible," he'd doubtless sneer. "You're a full-blooded Jew. You only need be one-fourth Jew to be arrested. You're not a Christian. You're a Jew, a *Büdös Zsidó*."

2

Enter George

Beginning classes at Zsidó Leany Gymnasium was exciting for me. Papa bought a house — butcher shop at Conti Utca 1 in Budapest so I could be near the tram for a quick ride to school. Our home was small but adequate, much like the homes of our friends. I slept on a cot at the foot of Mama and Papa's bed in the only bedroom. Jules slept on a daybed in the living room and Alex had a cot behind a curtain hung at the end of that room. Our maid (who freed Mama to work in the shop) set up a cot in the kitchen each night.

My first day of school I proudly wore my new uniform with its cap and embossed insignia, but my pride was short-lived. I quickly found that my uniform marked me as a Jew. Many days I would walk a half hour to school rather than endure the taunts on the tramway.

"Büdös Zsidó!"

The school itself was quite large and the work demanding. Boys and girls were kept strictly segregated; they even had separate entrances. Still I liked school and enjoyed its challenges, especially trying to keep my grades up with my brother Jules. My cousin Klara was one year ahead of me, and she delighted in teaching me all the things I needed to know.

Even so, when summer came, I welcomed it. Klara and I went swimming every day at Szechenyi Bath Resort. To us, clutching our towels and bag lunches, these trips were high adventure.

One day, while Klara and I were tossing a ring back and forth in the water, a boy kept leaping into the game, intercepting the ring every time I threw it.

He was Peter Schuck and he quickly became my boyfriend. For two years we saw each other several times a week without my parents' knowledge. They felt I was too young to date even someone as nice and handsome as Peter. I just didn't agree.

The 1936 Olympics were being held in Berlin at this time, and we Hungarians were excited and proud. Hungary placed third overall. Especially satisfying was the victory of Attila Petschauer, a fencer and a Jew. His gold medal irritated Hitler much as did those of the American, Jesse Owens.

Between school and Peter, my time passed rather pleasantly. The year 1938 came, and Hitler annexed Austria. While Hungarian Jews still hoped we would escape any such Nazi takeover, to me at fourteen these international occurrences were only a vague threat. Of far greater importance was the fact that Peter had dropped me. He had gone away for the summer and written me only one card. I was brokenhearted and disgusted as only a fourteen-year-old can be.

After a proper period of mourning, I decided to call my school friend, Martha Fischer. One of her five brothers, George, the skinny one, answered.

"Who is this?" he asked.

"Mari Komlos. Is Martha there?"

"Why do you want to speak to her?"

"I beg your pardon?"

"Why do you want to speak to her?"

I cleared my throat. I hadn't realized that George was so pushy. "I want to ask what her plans are for tomorrow, St. Stephen's Day. I'd like to meet her somewhere."

"And where is that?"

"I thought we might go to Margarite Island to swim."

"Well, I'll give her the message, but I might come myself."

I went alone to Margarite Island the next day and found George waiting for me on the dock. He looked like a young Ghandi, sitting there in his swimming trunks.

George fascinated me. He was nineteen to my fourteen, a quiet man, and a challenge. I had to keep asking questions to get him to talk. When he did speak, I was wise enough to listen, and I soon learned he was quick and intelligent. He just didn't share my tendency to tell the world everything.

George had been in Vienna the past winter, studying at the university. He had been there in March when Hitler and the Nazis occupied the country.

"I stood on the balcony of my room, Mari, and watched this little man parade triumphantly through Vienna. The crowds were cheering and the soldiers goosestepping. I kept marveling that this one man could manipulate history so." He shook his head wonderingly. "All schools were immediately closed to Jews, of course, and I came home."

"Did you mind terribly?"

He shrugged his shoulders impassively. "I decided not to waste my energy being bitter. There's nothing I can do to change the situation."

"At least you had a good job to come home to in your family's textile plant."

His face remained expressionless except for an eyebrow quirk. Did that mean he was amused at my juvenile attempt to comfort him or that he resented my platitude? I felt I had to find out. I had to know more about George Fischer.

3

English, Photography, and Meat Packing

My unexpected date with George developed into a six-year courtship. It was a classic case of opposites attracting. He challenged and charmed me with his quiet, serious demeanor. I was talkative, precocious, and full of energy, all my emotions very near the surface. George was deep and calm, with rarely a ruffle in the face he showed the world.

Mama and Papa were not aware of my affection for George. His frequent presence at our house was assumed to be related to his friendship with my brothers. Since George rarely spoke and I was not about to declare myself to my parents, Mama and Papa had no way of knowing the truth.

George was from an Orthodox family, though he was not a religious Jew himself. He was rebelling against the strictures of the Law. Still he, like all of us Jews, was concerned about what was happening to Jews all over Europe, especially since Germany was continually drawing Hungary into its circle.

Hitler's major ploy was to promise the return of all the lands taken from Hungary in the Treaty of Trianon in 1920, the settlement meted out on Hungary for her Central Powers activities during World War 1. In 1939, the Hungarian Regent, Admiral Miklos Horthy, signed the Berlin Pact with Germany, Japan, and Italy, making

us — along with Rumania, Bulgaria, Slovakia, and
Croatia, — a satellite of the three major Axis powers.
Hitler duly returned parts of Slovakia and Transylvania
as well as other territories to Hungary.

Unlike the leaders of the other Axis countries, the
Hungarian Horthy was moderate in his anti-Semitic feelings. He did oversee the development of forced labor
camps for Jewish young men, but at this time, 1940, the
men were properly clothed and fed. Alex and Jules and
George's brothers were impressed into these camps as
part of the slow, steady stream that bled the Jewish community of its youth and strength.

Though Hungarian Jews weren't suffering as the rest
of Europe's Jews, George decided that difficult times
were ahead. With the hope that the Allies would somehow beat the Nazis to Hungary, he began studying
English from a Berlitz book. During these early years
of the war, English lessons became a fad among Jewish young people, in a very real way our statement of
hope.

I had made previous attempts at mastering English
and had always failed. I determined to try again and
sought a tutor. I was sixteen when I met Mary Hajos.

Mary was a Jewess, but she was also a Christian, though
I didn't realize it at the time. She was an excellent teacher,
and I admired her. Often she asked me what I was
studying in my religion courses in school.

"Right now we're studying Isaiah," I told this little
blonde woman with the thick-lensed glasses.

"Then I have a suggestion," she said. "Why don't we
translate Isaiah 53 as a complement to your school
work?"

The translation was progressing well when suddenly
Mary surprised and upset me.

"Did you know," she asked, "that this One spoken of as

wounded for our transgressions and bruised for our iniquities is Jesus Christ, our Messiah?"

"No!" I was appalled. How could Mary even suggest such a thing! I knew the *Keresztenyek,* the Christians, believed that Jesus was somehow a god, but He was definitely *their* god.

It was like Papa always said. "We are Jews, Mari. Separate — and special."

"He's their god, Mary, not ours. He belongs to the *Keresztenyek* who persecute us."

"He's ours too."

"No!"

At school the next day I spoke to the rabbi about Mary's outrageous ideas concerning Isaiah 53.

"Don't let this woman's words upset you, Mari," he said. "This passage refers to the sufferings of the prophet himself or the nation of Israel, not the Messiah."

I took the answer back to Mary triumphantly.

She merely smiled and nodded. "I have heard this answer before."

Whenever my Scripture-based lesson gave her opportunity, Mary showed me other passages that she claimed referred to the Messiah.

During a lesson in which the reading dealt with King David, she might say, "Did you know that Jesus was a direct descendant of David? The Messiah will also come from the line of David."

I would run to the rabbi.

"How many descendants do you think David has?" he would ask.

I'd run back to Mary.

" 'Therefore the Lord Himself will give you a sign; Behold, a virgin shall conceive, and bear a son, and shall call his name Immanuel.' " she translated from Isaiah one day. "Jesus was born of a virgin."

"Yes, that's prophecy concerning the Messiah," said the rabbi. "But, Mari, that's not yet fulfilled. Messiah is not yet come. It is merely a *Kereszteny* legend."

"Mary," I asked my tutor in genuine wonder after a year of lessons, "how can you belive what the *Keresztenyek* believe? And if you believe as they do, does that make you a *Kereszteny*? Is your husband Emil a *Kereszteny*?"

"I cannot help but believe, Mari, and, yes, that makes me a *Kereszteny*. Emil also believes that Jesus is the Messiah."

"But Hitler is a *Kereszteny*, and so are his men and soldiers and all those who hate us!"

"No, Mari. They might not be Jews, but that are not *Keresztenyek* either. In Hungarian we have no word for people who are neither Jews nor Christians. English has a word, Gentile, but Hungarian does not. That's what these cruel people are, Mari, Gentiles. Not *Zsidó*. Not *Kereszteny*."

As I went back and forth between Mary and the rabbi, a battle raged within me, fueled by my own doubts and my fear of death. Hitler was so near, such an imminent threat. If anything happened to me, I knew there was enough sin in my life to keep me from being accepted by God. Even though I lit the candles with Mama Sabbath eve after Sabbath eve and attended synagogue regularly, the question of sin continued to haunt me.

Each year on the Day of Atonement, I went to the synagogue with my parents to fast and pray for forgiveness. So it was prescribed by the law. But I kept wondering — what if I died before another Day of Atonement? What about those sins in between? My sins might not be horrendous in light of what was going on the world about me, but they were my sins — my wrong actions or words or thoughts — and they plagued me. I had a keen sense of my fallibility and God's infallibility.

Mary said that if I believed in Jesus as my Messiah, my sins would be forgiven me forever. How could I know if she were correct? I was seventeen-years-old and very confused. All my preconceived ideas were being challenged, and I had no answers.

When I graduated from the *gymnasium*, I became a photographer's apprentice at the Margit Toth Studio in Budapest. My mornings were spent at her studio learning photography techniques and processes, and I found I delighted in both the artistic and functional aspects of what I hoped would be my career.

I knew I was very fortunate. Opportunities for Jewish young people were severely limited. We were not allowed to go to the universities, and apprenticeships were usually too expensive to buy. Though Margit Toth was not a Jew, she sympathized and allowed me to study with her.

My apprenticeship lasted a year. When I passed my exam, Margit hired me as an assistant photographer.

At the same time I was studying with Margit Toth, I was also apprenticed to my father because he felt we should all know the family business. I spent part of each afternoon at our butcher shop with its great entrance doors so large that I could barely manage them. Horse-drawn wagons delivering meat to be butchered entered through these doors.

Nearest the doors was the glass-enclosed cashier's booth where Mama sat, collecting money as noted on the slips of paper given each customer by the butcher.

My cousins Imre and Feri worked behind the booth cutting meat or stuffing sausage from a huge pile of ground meat beside them. Other workers would be lined up behind a long table, cutting and chopping according to Papa's instructions.

Next, in the smoking area, a big pot hung over a burning pile of wood, cooking the meat prior to smoking.

The smoking room itself was aromatic with the scent of slowly burning wood, its smoke rising to preserve the meat hanging from the ceiling.

Across the courtyard was an immense walk-in refrigerator in which Alex once locked himself. He was almost hoarse from singing to keep his spirits up when we found him.

Through the year of my apprenticeships, I continued my English lessons with Mary Hajos. George began formal lessons, too, scheduling his time with Mary immediately after mine. I would wait for him, and we could go out without having to tell anyone.

It wasn't long before Mary began talking with George about the Messiah.

"What did you say when she told you that Jesus was a descendant of David?" George asked me. "Surely in the two years you've taken lessons from her she's mentioned this idea to you?"

"Many times. I just told her what the rabbi said, that there are lots of descendants of David.

"Then what did you say when she told you that Jesus was born of a virgin?"

"I told her the Messiah would be, not Jesus."

For two more years this highly repetitious exchange went on. Mary would question me; I'd question the rabbi; I'd give Mary his answer; Mary would question George; George would ask me; I'd give the rabbi's answer; George would repeat the rabbi's answer. We were talking in circles, but we were also thinking.

Originally George was totally unimpressed with Mary's ideas, but slowly he began to wonder if perhaps she weren't correct after all. So many prophecies were fulfilled in Jesus, too many for mere coincidence.

"Mari, what if Mary's correct?" George asked after we left our lesson one night in the summer of 1943. "What if Jesus is the Messiah?"

"Do you actually believe He is?" I asked. I had never heard him so questioning before. He usually kept his thoughts to himself.

He shrugged his shoulders. "I don't know. But have you considered what believing might mean to us?"

"Salvation. Forgiveness."

I frowned as George shook his head.

"That's not what I mean," he said. "I was thinking about our parents."

I took a deep breath and let it out slowly. "I've thought about that, too. Do you think they'd be very upset?"

"I've known orthodox families to *sit shivah* for just such a reason," he said, referring to the tradional seven-day mourning ritual that follows the death of a close relative.

"Mama and Papa'd never do that!" I couldn't imagine their being that rejecting of me.

"I'm not so certain about my parents." George looked up at the night sky visible above the shops and homes of Budapest. "After all, they blame the Christians for the plight of all of Europe's Jews. They think Hitler's a Christian, just like I used to. If I became one of these same Christians . . ." His voice died on the question. "I don't know what they'd do."

One day Mary invited us to a Bible study she was having in English. I went primarily to improve my language skills, but I also wanted to show off my great knowledge of Scripture. The discussions were stimulating and disturbing.

As the battle I was fighting intensified, so did the world's. The Hungarian government was in turmoil. The persistent pressure from Hitler for Admiral Horthy to appoint more pro-German, anti-Semitic officials made it appear that if the Allies didn't attack us eventually, the Germans would. Caught in this political dilemma, in 1943 the government of Hungary began microfilming its records for safe-keeping, and I got a job helping. It was tedious, demanding work, but I liked the challenge.

My brother Alex was home from his labor camp at this time, having been discharged after more than a year of service. He helped me with the microfilming and I enjoyed his teasing, pleasant company.

Incredibly, my five-year romance with George blossomed beneath my father's unsuspecting eye. George's reticence and Papa's early evening bedtime combined to keep our secret.

But it was inevitable that eventually we would give ourselves away. After all, Papa was not foolish, only trusting.

After one of George's visits, Papa called me into the bedroom. He sat amid the covers, much sterner than usual, staring at me.

I stood at the foot of the bed, my heart beating wildly.

"Explain, Mari."

"We plan to marry, Papa." It was all I could force out.

Papa looked stunned. "You and that skinny boy? He doesn't even greet me when he comes in!"

"He's just quiet, Papa."

"I thought he came here to see your brothers. All these years it's been to see you?"

I nodded.

"I thought Pista was your boyfriend."

"No, Papa. George."

He looked at me closely, and my face must have revealed my heart.

He sighed, "You know best, dear." He lay back on his pillows.

How I loved Papa.

4

A Messiah and an Invasion

One by one, George's brothers had been drafted into forced labor, as had Alex and Jules. Mother and Father Fischer were concerned about George and the labor camps because George had been a sickly child. They were certain that the rigors of camp life would be too demanding for him.

When the fact that George was needed to help run the family textile business was no longer sufficient to exempt him from the draft, Father Fischer found a cooperative physician who was willing to give George a health deferral. Eventually even this ploy was not enough, so George developed "arthritis" of the knee.

Each week he would go to the clinic of a sympathetic doctor for a treatment which consisted of releasing a swarm of bees on George's knee to sting it until it swelled terribly.

I would go along with George and sit next to him as the bees did their work.

"Think of something else," I'd plead foolishly, tears in my eyes as he grimaced with pain.

As he limped beside me on our walk home, I'd ask, "Isn't there any other way?"

"Can you think of one?" he asked through pain-clenched teeth. "I can't."

Nor could I. It was 1943, I was nineteen, and the world

had gone mad. A little mustachioed man in Nazi Germany played a vile and vicious tune, and we all danced however reluctantly. I clung to George's hand, frustration and fear threatening to overwhelm me.

About this time, Alex came home on furlough from his labor camp, and we learned that conditions had deteriorated rapidly. His stories of his life over the past two years were tragic, and though he tried to act like the same carefree Alex who had left us, he had been changed.

"What did they make you do in camp?" I asked him.

"Promise you won't laugh, but since I had worked in a meat packing plant, they put me in the kitchen. I never want to peel another potato as long as I live."

"At least you had plenty to eat," I said, wanting to encourage him as he had encouraged me over the years.

He nodded. "I definitely had a better job than the poor devils who dug trenches for the Germans during those atrocious winters."

"You were in Russia?" I was appalled.

His eyes looked through me to things only he could see. "You know, the winter was our greatest ally. The Germans had never experienced anything like it and they were completely unprepared for it. They were defeated by the cold, darkness, and snow — and the persistent Russians."

We were sitting in our apartment, warm and comfortable, but unconsciously my brother pulled his sweater closer about himself.

"Thank God the troops I was assigned to were in Kurks on the River Don, not in Stalingrad. When the Russians retook that city, all foreigners were killed, whether German or interned Jew."

"What happened after the Germans lost in Russia?"

"We retreated."

I smiled. He had escaped the worst part of the devastation then. My smile faded abruptly as he continued to talk.

"The weather was absolutely brutal, as was the temper of the Germans. Everything was disorganized. There were few or no supplies. We walked — in the middle of winter — across the Ukraine and Poland. Men froze to death as they marched."

"Oh, Alex!"

"Back in Poland, men were housed in Dorosic, a camp for typhoid victims. I caught the disease as did many of the others."

He smiled at my horrified expression.

"Don't worry, Mari. Obviously I survived." He shrugged his shoulders. "Many didn't, of course. If the typhoid didn't get them in their weakened condition, then the fire that burned down most of the camp did."

"Oh, Alex!" I repeated. I could think of nothing else to say.

"Remember Attila Petschauer, the fencer?"

"The Olympic gold medalist? Certainly."

"He was in Russia at Kurks in a forced labor group like mine. I used to see him every day when he came through the lines in the mess hall. Then one day he didn't come. I asked about him, and one of the cooks in his group told me what had happened. The Germans forced Petschauer to climb a tree. Then they turned hoses on him until he fell, frozen to death, to the ground."

Such stories appalled me. How could people do such cruel, such inhumane things to each other? What if something horrible like that happened to someone I knew and loved. What if Jules were suffering some such horror right now? We had heard nothing from him for over a year.

Oh, God, take care of my family. Please!

I found less time to give my photography. As more

young men went to labor camps, Papa couldn't find workers, and I had to help him in the store. Jews were no longer allowed to own their own firms, so we had a straw man running our business, a Gentile Papa had hired to be (on paper) head of the meat market.

As things worsened in Hungary for us Jews, we hoped more than ever that the Allies would somehow rescue us. How could they not win with the resources of the United States behind them? With this hope ever before us, we continued with our English lessons with Mary Hajos.

"Listen to this," my persistent tutor said one night. " 'I am poured out like water, and all my bones are out of joint: my heart is like wax; it is melted in the midst of my bowels. My strength is dried up like a potsherd; and my tongue cleaveth to my jaws; and thou hast brought me into the dust of death. For dogs have compassed me: the assembly of the wicked have inclosed me: they pierced my hands and my feet. I may tell all my bones: they look and stare upon me. They part my garments among them, and cast lots upon my vesture.' "

Mary looked at me excitedly. "That's part of Psalm 22, and it speaks of the crucifixion of Jesus, Mari. It's a perfect description of that form of death. Yet when David wrote about it, men weren't killed that way. I believe God directed David to write."

"I'll talk to the rabbi," I said. But sometimes the rabbi couldn't help me that much.

"This psalm is symbolic, Mari, just symbolic. Don't you think you should find another English teacher?"

I often wondered that myself. But how many English teachers were there in Budapest, and how could I leave Mary with so many questions unresolved? Besides, I had developed a great affection for her.

"Look at this, Mari," Mary said another night. " 'For thou wilt not leave my soul in hell; neither wilt thou suffer thine Holy One to see corruption. ' That's Psalm 16. See how it was planned that the Messiah Jesus would not remain in the grave but would rise? This is one more Old Testament prophecy fulfilled in Jesus."

I didn't know what to believe. The rabbi, on one hand, had studied Scripture and was an authority. Mary, on the other, had a vast understanding of the Bible and seemed to know God Himself personally.

In the fall of 1943, I celebrated the Day of Atonement, as always. And, as always, the question of that 364-day gap before the next day when forgiveness was granted ate at me. I told Mary of my concern that I might die in the interim with unforgiven sin upon my soul.

She said, "Mari, Jesus died as our Paschal Lamb once for all. No guilty sins ever again, anymore. Forgiveness is total if you believe in Him."

Oh, God, what do I do?

During late 1943 and early 1944, we frequently met with a friend of Mary and Emil Hajos, a man named Imre Kádár. Imre was a Jewish believer from Transylvania who had fled to Hungary early in the war because of our relatively lenient national policies toward Jews. He filled his time by acting as a missionary to Hungarian Jews. He became to George what Mary had become to me, a spiritual guide and teacher.

The afternoon of March 8, 1944, George and I were at Mary's for our English lessons. After class we stood in Mary's living room talking with both Mary and Imre.

"What keeps you from accepting Jesus as the Messiah?" Mary asked us.

"Why don't you accept Him as your Savior?" Imre said.

These questions were not ones we could take to the rabbi. Ultimately we had to answer them ourselves. We found we had no more excuses, and we knelt together and accepted Jesus as the Messiah, our Savior.

When I got up from my knees where I had poured out my heart to God, I knew already that a change had taken place. The ever-increasing burden of questioning, and of seeking expiation and not finding it, of failing to measure up to the Law was gone. I felt I could fly.

I went straight home to tell Mama.

"Mama!" I shouted as I ran into our apartment. "Guess what? I've found the Messiah, Jesus Christ. I believe He died for my sins, and He's my Savior now."

Mama was stunned. When she found her voice, she said severely, "Mari, don't speak to me of this again. You are young yet. You will outgrow it. We will not speak of it again!"

A little over a week later Hitler called Admiral Horthy to Germany and issued an ultimatum: cooperate completely with me or be occupied. Horthy, who had tried to preserve some sense of Hungarian autonomy and control, agreed to cooperate. Even so, before Horthy's train returned to Budapest, German troops rolled into Hungary. Many moderate and liberal leaders were arrested, the government became very fascist, and the persecution of the Jews, which Horthy had held in check until now, began in earnest.

5

To the Ghetto

"George, wait a minute. I'd like to speak with you." Papa's big voice filled the apartment. George halted in the doorway.

I swallowed hard, knowing what was coming. Papa wanted to talk with George about his intentions toward me.

They walked down the steps and outside together. I watched from the window as they stood by the main gate and talked. I couldn't hear any of the conversation, but I could tell from Papa's face when he returned that George must have said the right things. At least my personal life was going well.

Since the invasion, German bombers had been making daily runs over Budapest. It made getting to and from work an exercise in fortitude.

One day I was half way home when the bombs began to fall. I rushed, terrified, to a shelter. As I listened to the explosions and felt the ground shaking beneath me, I pulled a small Bible from my purse.

I turned to Psalm 91 and read it. The words leaped out at me, and it was as though God Himself were speaking them aloud. I quickly looked up to see if anyone else had heard Him.

But everyone in the shelter was self-absorbed, either talking, playing cards, or staring into space. No one was paying the least attention to me.

I looked at the Psalm again.

"He that dwelleth in the secret place of the most High shall abide under the shadow of the Almighty.

"I will say of the Lord, He is my refuge and my fortress: my God; in him will I trust.

"Surely he shall deliver thee from the snare of the fowler, and from the noisome pestilence.

"He shall cover thee with his feathers, and under his wings shalt thou trust: his truth shall be thy shield and buckler.

"Thou shalt not be afraid for the terror by night; nor for the arrow that flieth by day;

"Nor for the pestilence that walketh in darkness; nor for the destruction that wasteth at noonday.

"A thousand shall fall at thy side, and ten thousand at thy right hand; but it shall not come nigh thee.

"Only with thine eyes shalt thou behold and see the reward of the wicked.

"Because thou hast made the Lord, which is my refuge, even the most High, thy habitation;

"There shall no evil befall thee, neither shall any plague come nigh thy dwelling.

"For he shall give his angels charge over thee, to keep thee in all thy ways.

"They shall bear thee up in their hands, lest thou dash thy foot against a stone.

"Thou shalt tread upon the lion and adder: the young lion and the dragon shalt thou trample under feet.

"Because he hath set his love upon me, therefore will I deliver him: I will set him on high, because he hath known my name.

"He shall call upon me, and I will answer him: I will be with him in trouble; I will deliver him, and honour him.

"With long life will I satisfy him, and shew him my salvation."

What indescribable comfort those words gave me. I

hugged to myself the promise that God would deliver us from the terror and pestilence all around us. I claimed this promise of safety not only for myself but for my family and George's family.

"Mama, look!" I showed her the Psalm as soon as I got home. "God has promised to keep us safe. Papa, look!"

They listened to me and read the Scripture, but it was love and pity for me, not faith in God's keeping power, that prompted their nods of agreement.

I knew my new faith in Jesus concerned them. They were hoping that my belief in Him would disappear, but with personal promises, such as Psalm 91, I could never go back to where I had been.

Shortly after the Lord gave me Psalm 91, we were forced to leave our apartment. Even though it was on the edge of the newly-established ghetto, no Jew was allowed to remain in his own home.

Some people, like Maca Fischer, George's sister-in-law, the wife of his oldest brother Leslie, chose to defy the orders and hide rather than go into the ghettos. Maca saw the future only too clearly in terms of collecting us and then exterminating us.

Since Leslie was in a labor camp in Russia, Maca hid with friends in the suburbs of Budapest. It was not long before she was found out and sent to Auschwitz.

For me, going to the ghetto was difficult. I had loved our butcher shop and home and there was a special wound in leaving this known, warm world and moving into a small apartment, twelve to a room, some of the twelve strangers. The Nazis understood all too well the demoralizing effect of displacement. The ghettos not only contained us; they stripped us of our individuality, our sense of ourselves, our feeling of controlling our own destinies.

Since the March invasion, we were no longer allowed

out of our homes without the yellow Star of David stitched on our coats. Everyone wearing the yellow patch was vulnerable to any type of harrassment with the attacker having no fear of punishment. While we found the ghettos like prisons, at least they were relatively safe.

Still not everyone turned against the Jews. Some cared and risked themselves to help us. Margit and Elek Toth agreed to keep our jewelry. Frauli, our former governess, took some of our things to her apartment.

Because she was married to a Jew, Frauli was especially sensitive to our situation. For a year her husband Leo had been hiding in their own apartment rather than go to labor camp. Because the authorities didn't search too assiduously, the deception had been successful. Whenever anyone came to the apartment, Leo lay on their bed and Frauli covered him with a hugh down coverlet that obsured any outline of his body. It was a severly restricted life, filled with constant terror, but Leo was still free.

In May, 1944, two months after the invasion, we heard the first rumors about young, unmarried Jewesses being taken for the pleasure of the German soldiers.

"George, what if they take me?" The thought made me sick inside.

"They'll never touch you, child," roared Papa. "I won't let them!"

"We'll get married immediately, Mari," said George quietly. "A big wedding after the war would have been nice, but we can't wait now."

I nodded as I bid farewell to my beautiful dreams. "When?"

We selected June 2, 1944, as our wedding date and began making what few plans we could.

George and I would live at Kőbánya, George's home, the site of Fischer Textiles. Father Fischer's business, spread out over five acres and employing approximately 500 people, made blankets. When the Nazis took Hungary, Fischer Textiles had been one of the first businesses they seized. They had retained Father Fischer as manager, and had confiscated all the blankets for wartime use.

The Fischers and all their Jewish employees were interned on the factory grounds in a miniature ghetto. In order to live there, I would have to work, too. My job would be sewing binding on the blankets. My home would be a small room set aside for just George and me.

As a special treat for our wedding reception, Mama asked Frauli to buy some petit fours for us. To Mama, these little iced cakes seemed to mean order and continuity in spite of the chaos, and she had her heart set on having them. Her only daughter's wedding would not be without some style, some beauty.

June 2 dawned, and we left early for the synagogue on Nagyfavaros Utca where we would meet George and his family and Rabbi Schreiber. Twice we were delayed for hours by air raids, and it was late afternoon when we finally arrived. Since we Jews were subject to a 5 o'clock curfew, time became very important.

Jewish law requires that there be a *minyan* or ten men present for every religious ceremony. Between our two families, we didn't have a *minyan,* so Papa went out into the street and impressed strangers as witnesses.

The ceremony took ten minutes. Instead of the beautiful gown I'd so often dreamed of, I wore bobby socks and an old dress. My veil was not yards of tulle but a paper napkin pinned to my hair.

"We are going to be late, Mama," said George to my mother after the service. "We must go directly to the factory, and we still may not beat curfew. I'm sorry."

Mama nodded, sad but resigned. Her petit fours would

have to wait. There was no order, no old way, no protocol in our present world, only chaos and broken dreams.

We kissed Mama and Papa goodbye and hurried to Köbánya, arriving late but without incident. After six years, I finally belonged to George.

6

An Unadorned Bride

"I have interesting news," said Father Fischer one night as we sat around the dinner table. "There is a way to avoid deportation."

Since the March invasion Jews by the thousands were being gathered up and set off to fates we could only imagine, many, like Maca Fischer, to an obscure place called Auschwitz in Poland.

Before the war, an estimated one in twenty Hungarians was a Jew, and refugees from all over war-torn Europe had increased the Jewish population beyond that. Now thousands of these people were disappearing, especially in the country, including my cousin Magduska.

Magduska had been living with Mama and Papa and me before the invasion, studying in Budapest. Suddenly Jews could no longer attend any schools.

"I'll go home to Nemeske if I can't study any longer," Magduska said.

"Don't go," we all urged her. "It's safer here in the city."

"No. Here there is turmoil. At home, all is peaceful."

We pleaded, but Magduska was insistent. She returned to her village of Nemeske.

One week later, in early April, the Arrow Cross, the forceful Hungarian Fascist corps, swept down on Nemeske and carried off every Jew in the village. We never saw Magduska or any of her family again.

41

"We can avoid being sent to labor or concentration camps?" I asked Father. I was delighted. George and I had been married about three weeks, and I never wanted to be separated from him again.

Mother Fischer nodded. "I've heard about this, too. If we are willing to let ourselves be called Christians," she almost shuddered, "we can be spared."

"What Mother means," said Father, "is that if we have a baptismal certificate, we can claim conversion. But we must have the certificates."

George was incredulous. "And the Nazis will honor them?"

"Remember," said Father, "this is Budapest, with its embassies and politicians. Even the Nazis want to impress the world favorably."

"Especially if they're losing," said George cynically.

"Father Josef, a priest friend of Papa's, could get us the certificates, I imagine," I said. "He's often offered to help us any way he could."

"I know it's necessary," said Mother, "but I hate lying and calling myself a Christian. After all they've done to us!"

George and I looked at each other.

"Well, Mari and I won't have to lie exactly," began George. He hadn't told his parents of his conversion yet. Because they were Orthodox Jews, he knew they would be more distressed than my family had been. He feared they would declare him dead as many Orthodox families did to relatives who became Christians.

When George hesitated, I spoke up. His fears didn't bother me. No one had ever rejected me personally before, and I couldn't imagine it happening now. "We wouldn't have to lie at all. We are Christians. We believe Jesus is the Messiah." I grinned. "We shouldn't have any trouble at all getting the certificates."

No one smiled back at me, and I was suddenly conscious of the strained stillness in the room.

"George," Father said harshly. "What is this?"

George looked unhappy. "It's true, Father. Mari and I are Christians. We have accepted Jesus as our Messiah and Savior."

Mother recoiled and put her hand to her mouth to stifle a scream.

"I forbid it!" said Father sternly.

"It is done, Papa," said George. "You can't forbid it. A person must believe what is right."

"And becoming a Christian is right?" Father jumped up from his place. "How could you do this to us? Don't you understand that it is the Christians who are persecuting us?"

"No, Father," George began. "It's — "

"Silence! I will hear no more. You are no son of mine if you believe in Jesus."

"Father!" I was horrified at his words, at their implication.

Mother nodded in agreement with Father. "Go to the people who taught you these things and let them take care of you. Go, both of you."

George rose slowly from his chair, stricken. "Do you mean what you say?"

He searched his parents' faces and saw the implacable strength of their orthodoxy.

I cried as we packed our few belongings. "George, what will we do? We can't go to Mary and Emil Hajos. The authorities would never allow it."

"I knew they'd be angry," George said. "That's why I didn't tell them. With everyone gone but me, I didn't want to hurt them more." He sighed. "I guess I always knew this would happen."

He was so sad, so hurt. I felt bewildered. I hugged my new husband, wanting to ease his pain.

"We knew the cost when we believed," I said. "I guess I never understood that we might actually have to pay it."

"It's worth the price," said George sadly. "Salvation is worth the price. Think what the Messiah paid — His life."

I nodded. "We can go stay with my parents; they'll take us in."

While Mama and Papa were glad for our company, it was a difficult time for George.

"Could we have done anything differently?" he asked many times. "Could we have avoided hurting them?"

"You had to tell them sometime, George. You couldn't deny the Messiah."

George nodded. Still, knowing he was right in declaring his faith didn't eliminate the pain of the estrangement.

Five long, prayer-filled days passed when suddenly we received a summons from Father to return.

"You are my son," Father said to George. "Sometimes I'm not so proud of you, but you are my son. Your brothers are all in forced labor; I need you at the factory. Also, in a time when literal death is too real, we cannot send a son to spiritual death."

George smiled and began to speak. Father raised a hand to silence him.

"Let me finish. You have done a terrible thing, George, to deny your heritage. We are appalled, but we have agreed to have you here if you will never speak of this again. Never. Do you both understand?"

We nodded. Things were not resolved as we would have wished — already we were praying for all in our families to find our Messiah — but at least the terrible rift was partially closed.

We slipped quickly into a routine at the factory. The war was at its height, and air raids were as much a part of our lives as sewing, weaving, folding, and sorting blankets.

When the siren sounded, day or night, we ran to the

shelter Father had built. Mother always carried a satchel with her in which she'd collected her valuables. She kept this satchel hidden under the sofabed on which George and I slept. At the first sound of the siren, she was there to get it, sometimes before I was even out of bed.

Summer came, and between the heat of working on the third floor of the factory, the smells of the factory, and the constant tension of the air raids, I often felt faint. I was surprised at myself and this new weakness. Many times I would run quickly to the bathroom to vomit. I caught people looking at me pityingly.

They understood before I that I was pregnant.

To be pregnant in a besieged city in wartime was considered folly.

"Get an abortion, Mari," people told me. "This is no time to be pregnant. George can't escape labor camp forever. You'll be left alone and you many never see him again. Winter is coming and things will be very difficult. Don't make survival any harder."

I refused to listen to such advice.

"No abortion," I said emphatically. "God will take care of me and the baby." I clung to that belief tenaciously.

In early Octorber, 1944, George finally got his orders to report to a collection point thirty miles north of Budapest for departure to forced labor. We said goodbye at the house, not wishing to reveal our emotions to the uncertain climate of the public train station.

I went to live with Mama and Papa, telling myself that others had survived separations; I would too. After all I had my memories, my Messiah, and my baby for comfort.

7

An Aborted March

There was a knock on the door one evening. I opened it, and there stood my husband.

"George!"

He stepped in quickly. "Hush, Mari. Don't tell the world. I'm not supposed to be here."

I clung to him. "How long can you stay?"

"Only tonight."

"Only tonight! But at least you are here. What are you doing in Budapest?"

"They needed workers for a job here, so I volunteered. I was able to get a night's pass to my parents' place. They told me you were here."

Mama put out some soup for George, and Papa tried to find a place for us to sleep. Sharing our reunion with the other eleven in our ghetto bedroom was impossible.

There was a tiny maid's room, more like a closet, off the kitchen. Papa persuaded the couple who used it to give it to us for the night.

I didn't want to sleep, to miss one minute of my short time with George. I couldn't believe he was actually here, even when I felt the firmness of his body beside mine.

Too soon it was dawn and George had to go. I fixed him breakfast and watched him eat. Before the sun was completely up, he left. My eyes filled with tears as I watched him, so thin and alone, walking away to an unknown future. I could do nothing but commit him to God. *For he shall give his angels charge over thee, to keep thee in all thy ways. They shall bear thee up in their hands, lest thou dash thy foot against a stone.*

Throughout the late summer and early fall, our fears for ourselves, for George, for Alex and Jules, increased daily. We heard rumors of unbelievable cruelty, of massive roundups, of men and women too weak to march being shot in the neck and left for the Hungarian peasants to bury, of whole villages disappearing.

One cheering piece of news was that Rumania had fallen to the Russians in August. We prayed Hungary would be next. Even the Russians were better than the Nazis.

As our nation's losses of men and supplies increased in the vain attempt to save the Reich, Admiral Horthy decided it was time to find new allies. In October he signed a preliminary armistice with Russia, and on October 15, 1944, he issued a proclamation of intent to surrender to Russia. He received no backing from his own army, and Germany responded to Horthy's turncoat policies by occupying Budapest with a panzer force.

Ferenc Szalasi, the leader of the strongly anti-Semitic, green-shirted Arrow Cross, assumed power. Instead of concentrating all his forces on resisting the Russians, he determined — for the second time — to solve the Jewish problem before the Russians arrived.

It had been Szalasi's Arrow Cross troops who had led the spring offensive against Hungary's Jews. They had rounded up thousands, including our Magduska, before Horthy had been able to halt them. At that time Budapest's Jews had been saved, but now Szalasi was loose once again.

One day an order was issued that all Jewish women in our ghetto between the ages of 15 and 45 were to report to the square in the morning. The only exceptions were those in the advanced stages of pregnancy or those with babies under a year. As usual the Nazis were showing their hypocritical chivalry about those they were going to march off to death.

Since I was not very pregnant, at dawn I packed my straw bag with a toothbrush, a change of clothes, my Bible, and my pictures.

Mama and Papa waited at the door.

"My little Mari," said Papa as he laid his hand gently upon my head.

"Papa!" My arms strained to encircle his bulk. His heart beat sounded strong and steady in my ear. How I longed for him to be able to lift me safe in his arms as he had done when I was a child.

Mama held me and wept softly. I was the third child she had had to send away, and she ached with physical agony in bereavement and fear.

We were certain we would never see each other again.

As we women gathered in the square, the brilliant sunshine mocked us and our fears. Many of my friends and former classmates were there. Beside me was Edith Grossman, the chief rabbi's daughter. We talked quietly, trying to hide our terror, until the soldiers began dividing us into two lines.

"You, over there," a soldier said to Edith, pointing with his finger where he wanted her to go.

"You," he paused as he looked at me. I was only four months pregnant, but very obviously so. I am small-hipped, and I carried my baby thrust forward. "You're too far advanced," he said. "Go home."

I stared at him, overwhelmed. I stood beside another girl, also saved by an advanced pregnancy, and watched as Edith and the others marched off. We never saw any of them again.

As I walked home, I was struck by the fact that the baby people had wanted me to abort had just saved my life. Surely God had something special for this little one. I rested my hand lovingly on my stomach.

Mama and Papa welcomed me back as though from the dead. Now, less than a month later, I was facing death again here on the racetrack with people the Nazis felt were the culprits of history, the dregs of humanity. The dregs? Not Mama and Papa. Not me. Not these Jews here with me. We might not be Aryans, but we weren't dregs. Jesus, the Messiah, had come from Jewish loins. We Jews were special, a chosen people.

I shivered and shifted my weight, feeling anything but special. My movement brought a sharp thump of protest from the baby. I was suddenly overcome with grief, convinced that my child would never be born.

"Are you all right?" asked Mama with great concern.

Her unselfish worry shamed me. I forced myself to smile. "I'm fine, Mama. The baby just moved."

We watched the soldiers pacing nervously in the bleachers. Soon it would be completely dark, and they were apprehensive about keeping so many prisoners under control at night. I listened grimly as some around me plotted escape. I felt that with so many armed guards about that any such venture was doomed. Better to stay here and hope. For some reason they hadn't killed us yet. Maybe they still wouldn't.

"Don't worry. The Russians will save us," said someone, as if wishing would make it so.

Darkness fell, and I went to sleep leaning against Papa. I awoke much later to the sound of someone screaming.

8

Protection Letters, Flimsy Lifelines

It had begun! The massacre had begun. I grabbed Papa's arm, terrified.

The screams continued, but they didn't spread across the crowd like I anticipated. Nor did I hear any shots.

I listened more closely.

"Can't we find a blanket? Some water?"

"Are you serious? Relax. It'll be all right."

"Relax? That's my daughter!"

I suddenly realized that I was listening to the screams of a young woman having her baby right here in the cold of night at the racetrack.

My hands went instinctively to the large curve of my own body. I shivered.

Dear God, where will my baby be born? Will he even have a chance to be born, or will he be killed here with me today?

Mama slipped her arm around me and patted me comfortingly.

Eventually I fell into a fitful sleep, only to awaken at dawn stiff and hungry. It had been a long time since yesterday's breakfast.

Static crackled over the public address system. Everyone froze in an attentive, apprehensive tableau.

"Line up by threes," a cold voice told us. "Line up for the march back to Budapest."

We hugged each other in joy. They were going to take us home! It made no sense to me that they had marched us out here and held us over night only to release us. I couldn't understand why they hadn't killed us when they had the chance, but I thanked God for my life.

I certainly didn't know, but I thanked God for my life.

Back in the ghetto again, time hung heavily. There was very little to do, and there was no privacy. Fear lived with each of us, and anger and frustration. The soldiers patrolled our streets, harrassing, bullying, and sometimes beating people for no apparent reason. We knew no safe place.

My body continued to grow and my clothes were now too tight for me. I felt like buttons and zippers would never close again.

One day there was a knock on the door. It was Frauli.

"Here," she said. "For you."

She put a large piece of heavy navy blue material in my arms.

"You need a maternity dress."

"Oh, Frauli, to risk your life for such a thing!" I hugged the material happily. How warm it would be in the coming winter months. "It will probably be my only one."

"How's Leo?" asked Papa of Frauli's husband. We were standing in our crowded living room, trying to have a private conversation while people we barely knew listened, if only to allay their boredom.

"Fine. Bored. He's still hiding." She shrugged her shoulders. "At least I know where he is."

How fortunate she is, I thought. I had no idea where George was. All I could do was pray and commit him to God.

"I can't stay long," said Frauli, "but I thought you'd like to know what happened when you were marched to the racetrack." She took a deep breath and looked with compassion at each of us, Mama, Papa, and me. "The plan was to shoot you all."

I nodded, remembering the machine guns that had been aimed at us and didn't doubt her at all.

Frauli continued. "Count Raoul Wallenberg, the Swedish diplomat here in Budapest, somehow heard of the march and convinced the Nazis that it wouldn't look good to the world community if all of you were killed."

"The Nazis are careful to perform their atrocities in secret," said Papa caustically.

"I've heard of Count Wallenberg," I said. "Isn't he the man responsible for saving the lives of many Hungarian Jews?"

Frauli nodded. "Wallenberg seems to have made the Jews his cause. He's a skilled mediator. Even Szalasi listens to him, or so it seems. The man's risked his life a number of times by confronting the authorities and demanding the release of Jews. Once he even chased a trainload of deportees in his car, jumped aboard near the border, and talked the guards into releasing all the prisoners who had any papers, even if they were only birth certificates."

"I wish we had some logical connection with Sweden," said Papa. "It's a neutral country, and I understand that Wallenberg has issued provisional passports to Jews who have any commercial or personal connections with Sweden, and these passports protect the holders from the Nazis."

Frauli smiled. "Haven't you heard? He's also issued over 5000 certificates of protection available to anyone. The Swiss have followed his lead and issued a large number too."

"I have one question," said Mama, folding her arms over her ample bosom. "Why are the Nazis respecting these pieces of paper?"

Papa shrugged. "They don't want bad world press. Since Budapest is the country's capital, many foreign reporters and diplomats serve here. Also they can't afford to anger the neutrals. Remember, they're losing the war."

"Wallenberg has made such an issue of your safety that the world is literally watching," said Frauli. "You can thank God it's 1944 instead of 1940."

After Frauli left, we talked about our chances of getting protection letters. It was the first time we'd felt anything as concrete as hope for a long time.

Lord, can we avoid the inevitable after all?

Papa asked the advice of Dr. George Orban, a cousin of Mama's who was one of those who shared our apartment. As a physician, Dr. Orban was frequently called on by the Nazis to treat people outside the ghetto. On these professional visits he learned many things.

"Can you help us get these protection letters?" Papa asked Dr. Orban.

I held my breath as I waited for his answer.

Dr. Orban shook his head. "When the Nazis take me to treat someone, they keep me under close guard. They don't want to give me an opportunity to get such a letter myself."

"But they don't mind using your talents," said Papa disgustedly. "Hypocrites."

"There's got to be a way!" I cried. "We've got to get those letters."

"Easy, Mari." said Papa as he put his arms across my shoulders.

"You need to find a Gentile, Dezso," Dr. Orban said. "Someone who can move about freely and who's willing to risk getting the certificates for you."

"Lajos, the meat salesman," said Mama. "He always said he'd help us in any way he could." Lajos had worked for Papa for years.

"I'll try to contact him," said Papa, "but don't get too excited. We've no idea whether we'll be successful or not. Lajos might not want to get involved." In spite of his cautionary words, Papa's eyes gleamed with anticipation.

A few days later Lajos appeared at our door. He and Papa talked earnestly. They decided to try for letters of protection from the Swiss because their embassy was closest. Theoretically, less distance meant less potential trouble for Lajos.

"There are also protection houses," Papa told us after Lajos left. "Wallenberg first started them when he bought thirty-two apartment houses and opened them to anyone who had a Swedish protection paper. The Swedish flag flies over these houses and Wallenberg and his associates stand guard. The Swiss also have such houses. We will try to go to one."

Three anxiety-filled days later Lajos returned. Out of his pocket he pulled three folded letters. I stared at them, mesmerized. Such flimsy lifelines.

"How can we ever thank you for our lives?" said Papa, tears in his eyes.

"It is enough to know that you would have done the same for me," said Lajos. The men embraced and Lajos left.

The ghetto was now alive with purpose as everyone sought to secure a protection letter and people packed their scant belongings for the move to a protection house.

"Will these houses be better than what we have here?" asked Aranka Orban, Dr. Orban's wife. "Will they feed us, protect us? At least we know how things stand here."

"That we do," said her husband. "We know they are systematically emptying the ghettos, and that if we stay here, we are certain of dying. It's a risk to leave, yes, but less so than staying. Here we're all corralled like cattle waiting to be slaughtered. At least in those houses we have a chance."

Aranka nodded. Though she couldn't stop worrying, she understood. Leaving was a gamble, but staying was suicide.

I was more than willing to take the risk. If the move would give me a few more days or weeks of life, that was all I asked. My baby was active, often kicking me, always moving about. Every day I survived brought his birth that much closer.

One Thursday in the middle of November, we heard shouting in the courtyard.

"The guards are here to accompany all with Swiss protection papers to the Swiss safe houses. Prepare to show your papers."

Mama, Papa, and I quickly gathered our few belongings, said goodbye, and joined the line of people. I didn't know what awaited me, but I felt no sorrow in leaving the ghetto, only great anticipation.

9

But for the Grace of God

The shocking devastation of war was apparent everywhere as we walked through the streets. Windows were blasted out of bomb-damaged buildings and craters pocked the streets. The once lovely Budapest was a deserted wasteland with only soldiers and military policemen and an occasional beggar on the streets to see us marching to our protection houses.

We were in Pest, the half of Budapest on the east bank of the Danube River. It had once been an elegant area, only two blocks from the river. Now it was a ruin.

Swiss officials assigned us to a two-bedroom apartment in a minimally damaged modern building. We shared our rooms with forty-five other people, mostly strangers.

"Mama," I whispered, appalled, "this is worse than the ghetto!"

She waved me to silence, but disappointment was clear on her face, too.

A sign of the once elite stature of our apartment building was its central heating system, very rare in Budapest at this time. However, in keeping with the chaos of war, the system no longer worked, and even if it had, the absence of glass in all of our windows would have made it useless. The frigid air poured in unimpeded.

Joining us in our apartment was one family we knew, the Hegyis: Imre, his wife Ica, their daughter Duci, and their son-in-law, who was also my cousin, Imre Nemes, a strong healthy young man in his early twenties

"How does he happen to be here?" Papa asked, pointing to young Imre and thinking of Alex and Jules.

"He escaped from labor camp, and we're hiding him. We were even able to get a letter of protection for him." Mr. Hegyi looked around carefully as he talked. "But don't mention his escape. Some people will do anything for food or favors."

We nodded knowingly, though anyone who gave the situation any thought would surely conclude young Imre was an escapee.

As we began settling into our crowded quarters, we looked for food. There was none.

"Maybe Aranka Orban was right to worry about our being fed," I said, despondent over the state of the protection houses. I had dreamt lovely visions of privacy and order. Disillusionment burned like salt in a wound. "How will we get our food?"

In answer an official came to our door. In his arms he had a large can of lard and a jar of jelly.

"You will have to ration yourselves," he told us. "Each of you is to get a spoonful of lard and a spoonful of jelly daily. Appoint someone to be in charge of the distribution."

Lard, a pork product, and jelly!

"Every morning at 10 o'clock, you will get your allotment," Papa said. He and Mr. Hegyi were appointed to oversee our rations. "If any of you have brought food with you, it must be shared with the rest of us." He looked around the group, most of them people he didn't know. "I'm sure you realize that even if you have been able to remain kosher these past months, you must all eat the lard. There is no choice. Survival comes before ceremony."

Papa waited, but there was no disagreement.

"Mari, you have a watch. You will tell us when it is 10 o'clock."

I nodded, staring at the can and jar. All I could think of was Papa's freezer hung with meat.

As night came, people began to claim sleeping places. The Hegyi family and two or three others took the sofa bed, the only major piece of furniture in the place. The rest of us settled on the floor. My coat made a passable mattress. Next to me was Aniko Weisz, another of Mama's seemingly inexhaustable supply of cousins. All around us lay strangers, but we were all so weary we went to sleep quickly.

I awoke, cramped, in the middle of the night, and found I couldn't move. The press of people was so tight I couldn't even turn over. When I could stand it no longer, I nudged Aniko.

"Can you move a little so I can turn over?"

Aniko had no room either, so she nudged the person next to her who nudged the person next to her. Finally someone could move, and slowly, one at a time, people turned until finally Aniko and then I could move. The relief was marvelous.

The overcrowding, the boredom, and the disappointment that things weren't better made the days and nights endless.

We soon discovered that contrary to what we had been told, we weren't being guarded much of the time.

"Papa! Soldiers are coming!"

I was standing at our fifth floor window one day shortly after we moved in.

"Don't worry, Mari," Papa said. "Our guards will send them away."

"What guards?" I leaned out to see better the front of our building. "I don't see anyone."

Papa looked down, frowning. "They promised to protect us. Perhaps the guards are inside the lobby area."

They weren't. As we watched, the soldiers walked un-impeded into our quarters. We could hear them shouting and stomping on the floors below us.

"What do they want?" I whispered through stiff lips. "Us?"

But the soldiers never reached our floor, and in a short time they left our building, laughing and joking among themselves. They had no prisoners. They had been searching for the money and valuables they were convinced we had, not people.

These sudden invasions occurred without warning during the frequent intervals when we had no protection. Because we, as a family, had nothing to interest the soldiers, they affected us little. Actually they were less frightening than the ghetto raids because they rarely involved physical harrassment. We grew to accept them as another of a long line of inconveniences.

What we could not adapt to was the lack of purpose in our lives, the futility that came from day after day of enforced in activity. Sometimes I felt I'd go mad if I couldn't do something or go some place.

In the next room was a girl my age, Gabi. She was pleasant and pretty and somehow had gotten hold of false Gentile identity papers. One day as we talked during a lull in the bombing, we decided to use them, just to relieve the boredom and have an adventure.

"We can sneak out and visit friends on the outside," I said, eagerly.

"Maybe we can even find food," Gabi said. "Wouldn't that be wonderful?" Her face was alight with anticipation.

"Anything would be preferable to being held prisoner here," I said. "I'll go visit Frauli."

"I know someone who might be able to help all of us if I

asked. But we musn't tell anyone we're going. They'd only try to stop us."

I agreed.

The next morning we met at the front door. Gabi had two sets of identity papers with her, and she gave me one.

"Remember, Mari, you are now Magda Nagy. I'm Anna Toth. Let's meet at 3:30 at the tram stop."

We separated. As I made my way through the deserted streets to Frauli's, I began to feel frightened and uneasy. The closer I got to my destination, the more conspicuous I felt. People in this neighborhood knew me. What if someone saw me and reported me so that he could collect the bounty placed on Jews? I realized how foolish I had been to leave the protection house.

I breathed a sigh of relief as I entered the front door of Frauli's apartment building. I hesitated to be certain no one was around; I had no desire to make trouble for Frauli and Leo.

Across the courtyard on the third level I saw someone. My heart began to beat wildly, but as I watched, the person deliberately turned his back so he couldn't see me or where I was going.

I hurried to Frauli's door.

"Who's there?" she called out cautiously in answer to my frenzied knocks.

"Me, Mari."

She threw the door open and I fell into her welcoming arms.

She held me away from her, examined me carefully, but asked no questions.

"You look good. Too thin, but good."

"It's my dress," I said, smoothing down the heavy navy wool of my maternity dress with its expandable waist. "Thank you again."

Frauli smiled. She stepped to the door of the bedroom,

a small room filled with three beds, one for her, one for Leo, and one they rented for needed income. Each bed had a feather mattress and a down comforter.

"Leo, it's all right," she called. "It's just Mari."

I looked and saw no Leo.

Suddenly the comforter on one bed was thrown back and Leo emerged.

I laughed. "I couldn't even see the outline of your body, Leo. All those feathers make that an excellent hiding place."

After we talked for awhile, Frauli said, "Why don't you lie down and sleep? I'm sure a bed all to yourself would feel good."

She covered me with a down quilt as she had covered Leo.

In no time she was shaking me awake.

"You've been asleep 4 hours. You must go soon or you'll miss Gabi. But before you go, I've fixed a meal for you."

She led me to her small table where I found a delicious paprikas dinner.

"Where did you get that meat?" I asked, staring in disbelief.

"Never you mind. Just eat.

"Aren't you and Leo going to eat with me?"

She shook her head. "Not now. I'll just sit with you, and we can talk."

When I finished my feast, it was time for me to leave. I struggled into my coat.

"How are your rabbits?" I asked as I knelt by their cage near the door. "Oh, dear, there's only one left. I'm sorry. I know how you enjoyed them both."

Frauli smiled, and the truth hit me. My dinner! I was unable to speak as she handed me a jar of raspberry jelly, kissed me goodbye, and pushed me gently out the door.

"Come back whenever you can," she urged.

I met Gabi and listened to the story of her day, all the while warmed by the memory of Frauli's love and the marvelous sated feeling from the paprikas.

"Stop!" an authoritative voice commanded.

My stomach lurched. We had been so busy talking that we hadn't seen the military policeman approaching us.

"Your papers!" he ordered.

We were terrified and it showed. If only we didn't look so Jewish!

"Your papers! Now!"

What fools we had been. We had risked our lives for a lark, and now we were caught. Carrying false identity papers meant certain death.

The policeman seized Gabi's papers.

"Your name?" He stared at her.

She went white. She couldn't remember the name on her papers.

"You will come with me," the man said menacingly.

"No," she pleaded. "Please, no."

"Magda Nagy. Magda Nagy," I muttered over and over to myself. "Magda Nagy. God, help us!"

I waited in terror for him to turn on me. I rested my hand protectively on my stomach as if I could shield my baby from the danger.

The policeman never questioned me, never even talked to me. While I watched helplessly, he led the terrified Gabi away. She never returned.

As I ran home, trembling with each labored stride, I kept wondering why the policeman had been concerned only with Gabi. Was it because she was young and pretty and not pregnant? Had my baby again saved my life? Or did the man have a quota of arrests, and he needed only one more?

Whatever the reason, I knew God had protected me.

We had been fools, Gabi and I. Why God had saved me and not her, I didn't understand, but I knew it was only because of His grace that I had escaped. I certainly didn't deserve it.

10

Hiding Out

It was late November and the weather was becoming increasingly colder. The wind whistled through our apartment, wrapping in its drafty fingers our throats, our backs, our whole bodies. I dreamed of summer and of the warmth it would bring.

Each day was a curious contrast, tedious and boring, yet taut with tension. People sat in the apartment talking, playing cards, or just sitting and staring. The physical inactivity was frustrating, but with our lard and jelly diet, we hadn't much stamina anyway. Just the problem of forty personalities with their diverse needs and wants drained and challenged us all.

And beneath the day-to-day routine was always the ever present, crippling fear. Would today be the day? Or would we be fortunate and reach tomorrow?

God, You promised to keep us, to deliver us from the pestilence that walketh at noonday. Please, Lord, I'm depending on You.

One day there was a knock at the door.

"Is Dezsö Kombs here?"

"Imre Szabo!" Papa was floored to see his old friend from World War 1, the Hungarian Civil Policeman who had gotten me they hay to sit on at the racetrack. "What are you doing here?"

"I have found the young man I was to give this picture to." He held out the photo of me that I had given him at the Angyalföld racetrack. He has escaped from a labor camp and is hiding with his family in a factory in Angyalföld. Here are the directions."

With a singing heart I took the note. George was safe! I scarcely noticed Papa slip the messenger something.

"I'm going to him," I said.

"No," said Papa. "You're safe here. George is safe where he is. Soon the war will be over and you can be together again."

I shook my head. "No, Papa. I must go to him now."

He turned to Mama. "You talk to her. Tell her how dangerous it is. Tell her it's not right."

"Mari, think of the baby," said Mama. "You must not put it in danger."

"The Lord will protect us, Mama. I'm going tomorrow morning."

The next day I told Papa for the last time when it was 10 o'clock. I took my portion of lard and jelly and fervently hoped the Fischers had something else to offer me to eat. I put on my coat, took my little straw bag, and kissed Mama and Papa goodbye.

I set out on foot for Angyalföld, a suburb of Budapest. I hurried as quickly as I could, not wanting to be caught by either the bombs or the police.

I passed the Vigszinház, the famous Hungarian theater that was boarded up for the war, and turned the corner.

Suddenly there was a whistling sound and a great crash. A violent wind tried to blow me over.

I looked back over my shoulder and saw that the Vigszinház had taken a direct hit. Only a few yards had saved me from injury or death in the explosion. I wrapped my coat tighter about me and hurried on through the rain of bombs.

Finally, I reached Angyalföld and approached the

factory. It was surrounded by a great stone wall. How would I get in? How would I find George? Was it safe just to ask where he was?

I approached the gate. A sign said that this textile factory was working for the Hungarian-German government. Was I at the right place?

I took a deep breath and knocked.

"Who's there?" called a voice from inside.

"I am Mari Fischer, wife of George Fischer."

The door opened. A stranger who appeared to be a Gentile let me in.

"Follow me."

He led me past several small factory buildings, and I realized that this whole plant was specious. There was no weaving going on anywhere. I knew better, though, than to ask questions right now.

The man stopped in front of a door and opened it.

"George!"

I flew to him and felt secure in his arms.

"We've made it," I thought. "We'll be safe here until the war is over."

Suddenly I became aware of a wonderful aroma. Mother was boiling potatoes over a small can of sterno.

A potato! One whole potato every day, all for me!

"You don't know how delicious this is, Mother," I said as I savored its flavor and warmth. "After lard and jelly, believe me, this is a feast."

Our small room held eight of us: Mother and Father who shared a lower bunk; Leslie and Charles, George's brothers who, like him, had escaped their labor details and who shared a top bunk; Dávid and Anna Felseta, friends of the family and discoverers of this hiding place, who shared a lower bunk; and George and I who slept in an upper berth. It was all I could do in my rounded condition to climb up there, and I clung to George to keep from falling out.

"I feel so safe here," I said, looking around the little room.

"You shouldn't," said Father.

"Why not?"

"Because too much can go wrong too easily and too quickly."

"Father," said George, "you're a pessimist."

Father shook his head. "A realist," he corrected.

"How did you come to find this place?" I asked.

"One day the Arrow Cross came to Fischer Textiles for me. I escaped over the rear fence along with Leslie who had been hiding with us. My friend Janos Kohn had told me about Angyalföld, so we came here."

"And Mother?" I asked.

Father took a deep breath and exhaled slowly. "She and all the other women on the factory grounds were arrested and taken to the ghetto because the Arrow Cross couldn't find me. Two days later the whole apartment complex was force-marched to the Hungarian-Austrian border."

"That's 180 kilometers!" I said, aghast at the idea of such a march. Usually the nearest railroad was the destination.

Father took Mother's hand. "Many never made it," he said. "Any who faltered were shot."

I looked at Mother and recognized the same pained, inward look I'd seen on Alex's face when he talked about Kurks and Dorosici.

"I hired a Hungarian Nazi soldier to follow the marchers," said Father. "He caught up to them at Hegyeshalom at the border and brought Mother here to me. Then we wrote notes to all our children telling them where we were. And we sat back to wait."

I was amazed at Father's story.

"It's a miracle that we're here," I told George when we

were alone. "Only God could have gotten those notes delivered and us here."

He nodded.

"Where did the messenger find you?" I asked.

"In an old army barracks here in Budapest."

"You were right here the whole time?"

"No, not at all. I was always in Hungary, but usually I was around Vac, building pontoon bridges across the Danube for the Germans."

"Then how did you get to Budapest?"

"The Germans began concentrating hundreds of us. Usually they limited a work force to 50 to 100 so they could control us easily. Suddenly they stopped feeding us and began marching troops from all over to this barracks, amassing 1000 to 1500 of us."

I shivered. I knew only too well what that meant.

"I decided I didn't like the situation," said George in great understatement. He looked at me, eyes suddenly twinkling. "Poor toilet facilities."

I grinned and he grinned back. Waves of happiness washed over me. *Thank you, Lord, for bringing George back.*

"Anyway I decided to leave," said George. "If I stayed, it was certain death. If I left, the odds were more in my favor — only probable death."

My quiet, rational George made his logical decision. No panic, no hysteria, just a refusal to be slaughtered without some protest.

"Within ten minutes of my decision, I was walking along the fences surrounding the barracks. I pushed until I found a couple of loose boards. I shoved them aside and climbed out."

"Just like that?" I couldn't believe it.

"Just like that. I found myself on a side street. I walked to the main street at the end of the block and realized that I'd have to pass the front gate to get the tram to get here."

"But the guards!"

"I had to walk right past them. I just pulled up my collar, stuffed my hands in my pockets, and walked by. I ignored them and they ignored me."

"Oh, George, an angel must have blinded their eyes."

He nodded. "I certainly look Jewish enough. And my boots." He held out feet clad in heavy leather workboots reinforced with steel plates at the toes and insteps. "They are definitely prisoners' boots. We all had them. And noisy! You can hear them clomping for miles. I just thank God we were wearing our own clothes, not prison uniforms."

That night, snug in the little factory room with George at my side, I enjoyed the incredible luxury of a cup of camomile tea sweetened with a few grains of real sugar. I was overwhelmed at God's goodness to us. Finally our hard times were over.

It was a bruising jolt when Mr. Hasz, the Gentile guard, came to our room and said, "We must rig up a warning signal in case of a raid."

My euphoria fell away and reality returned. We were still at war.

"There is a buzzer in each room," Mr. Hasz continued. "I used to use it to signal lunch. If you ever hear it ring, hide as quickly as possible. I'll give you as much time as I can." He looked at our apprehensive faces. "I doubt I'll ever have to use it," he tried to reassure us.

Father grunted. Clearly he expected the alarm to sound any day.

Listening for the buzzer became our fulltime occupation. During the bombings, we would strain, listening for that raspy sound. Finally, about ten days after my arrival, it happened.

First, in the quiet of the early evening, we heard shouts and banging in the direction of the main gate. Then the buzzer sounded, echoing like an explosion through the little room.

We froze momentarily.

Then, "Follow me!" Father ordered.

"Where?" asked George.

"Just follow me!" Father was already out the door. We quickly obeyed, and he led us across an alley to the next building. Once inside, he began pulling away the planks of the wall under a staircase.

"In," he ordered.

We jammed ourselves in the dead space beneath the stairs, and Father pulled boards behind us, to close us in.

It was dark and eerie in our hiding place. I was afraid to breathe for fear someone outside might hear me.

As I stood motionless, trying to hear what was happening outside over the clamor of my hammering heart, I was filled with a sense of wonder. God had used Father's pessimism to keep us from the snare of the fowler and the terror by night. Father had searched out this little space for us, prepared it even to the building of two small benches we could take turns sitting on, and he had told no one for fear of his secret's being discovered.

Outside we could hear soldiers shouting and searching the grounds for the eighty or so Jews who were hiding here. We could hear screams and pleas for mercy. None of us dared move.

Gradually it became quiet. Then, just as I began to relax, someone raced by. I tensed, the blood roaring so loudly in my ears I was certain he could hear. Only a few thin boards separated me — us — from him.

Suddenly, Mother began to cough.

Father clasped his hand over her mouth and shoved her in a corner. The rest of us leaned on her to muffle the sound. We scarcely breathed while we waited to see if the coughs had been heard.

No one came.

As the night passed, our little cubby hole grew more and more stuffy. Not enough air crept in through the cracks in the boards to replace the depleted oxygen, and we became lightheaded. We leaned against each other for support.

Finally I could contain myself no longer.

"George," I whispered. "I have to go to the bathroom."

George talked quietly to Papa. It had been still for some time now, and Papa decided we could risk leaving our hideaway. He pulled aside first one, then another board. Outside there was only silence and darkness.

I slid out and George followed me. The fresh air felt wonderful as we hurried across the alley to our room.

When I came out of the bathroom, I said, "Can I lie down here for a while? I feel faint from standing."

He nodded and we lay down. I slept for perhaps an hour before he wakened me.

"It's almost dawn. We'd better go back now."

As we slipped across the alley, we met Mr. Hasz.

"You are still here?" he asked in surprise. "They got everyone else. Where did you hide?"

We showed him Father's place beneath the stairs.

Mr. Hasz nodded. "Stay here for today, but you'll have to leave as soon as possible. Once they raid a place successfully, they come back again and again to make certain there's no one else hiding there. It's too dangerous for you to stay any longer."

"But where will we go?" I asked.

"I'll try to think of something," he said.

We stayed in our hiding place all day, emerging only when necessary. Once Father slipped out to have a talk with Mr. Hasz. He had some money hidden which he hoped would encourage Mr. Hasz's speedy help.

"I'm suspicious of Hasz," said George after Father left.

"What do you mean?" I asked. "He's been more than helpful."

"But why is he still here? What usually happens to Gentiles who shield Jews?"

Charles and Leslie, listening to our conversation, drew their forefingers across their throats.

"Exactly," said George. "Unless there is some special reason not to harm him."

"Like if he's the one who reported us," said Leslie.

"Then how can we trust any help he'd get us?" I asked.

"We can't. But we have no choice," said George.

Father returned in an hour.

"Mr. Hasz has a friend who has found a bombed-out house for us to hide in. He will let us know when the arrangements are firm."

Later in the day Mr. Hasz came to us.

"My friend will escort you tonight. He knows of a ruin in Zugló where you'll be safe. He'll supply you with food."

Night came, and with it the man, a shadowy stranger to whom we were giving our lives.

"Follow me," he said.

Lord, I don't know where we're going, whether or not it's a trap. Lord, we're trusting ourselves to You.

After a walk of five miles, we came to the village of Zugló.

"There," said our guide, pointing to a pile of rubble that had once been a home. Only the basement and part of the bathroom remained. "Stay in the basement and you'll be safe. Here are a candle and food. I'll be back in a week with some more."

And he was gone.

We stumbled wearily down the steps.

Thank you, Lord. We're safe again.

11

Lice and Pickled Herring

Our hiding place was inky black, its only window boarded up. All I could tell in the darkness was that there was nothing to sit on, just a cold cement floor.

As I walked across the room, I stumbled over something in the dark. I bent down and touched it cautiously. It felt like a blanket.

"Look what I found!"

I picked up my treasure and discovered it was a heavy overcoat.

"Spread it out," said Mother. "We can share it."

"Here, I found another one," said Father, spreading his next to mine.

"Where do you think they came from?" I asked.

"Probably some soldiers hid here for some reason and left them," said Father.

"I wonder what caused them to leave in such a hurry that they left their coats?" I asked. "Bombs? The resistance? Their commander?"

We huddled together on the large woolen garments and slept.

When I awoke, it was morning. Light filtered through the boarded window, but still the cellar, the size of a small bedroom, remained largely in shadows.

"I'm going to light the candle for a while," said Father. "With the sun shining outside, no one will see it."

The candle only served to underscore the cheerless-ness of our hiding place. Our spirits were as gray and barren as our surroudings.

"At least we have food," said Mother.

She took the jar of food our guide had given us and turned it toward the light. In disbelief I read the label: Pickled Herring.

"Pickled herring? For a whole week? With nothing else?" My stomach curdled at the thought.

Carefully, mother rationed some of the preserved fish, and we ate the vinegary stuff. My mouth puckered.

"We need water," I said. "I hear dripping."

"I hear it too," said Father. "But it's too dangerous to explore before dark."

He blew out the candle and we sat in the deep shadows, watching the shafts of sunshine that peeked through the boarded window move leisurely across the floor. I de-spaired at time's slow passage.

Suddenly, I felt something crawl on me. I quickly brushed it off, but I felt it again almost immediately.

"George," I whispered, "there's something crawling on me." I shivered in revulsion as goose bumps rose on my arms.

"What is it?"

"I don't know." I brushed and brushed at my persistent visitor.

"If it doesn't bite, don't worry about it."

Calm, practical George. "But it gives me the creeps."

"What would you like me to do?"

"Make it go away! Ugh!"

Finally night came.

"Now we'll check for water," said Father.

We crept upstairs, and in the half blasted bathroom we found a toilet and a sink. The dripping we had heard was from the sink.

"We can use the toilet if we don't flush it," said Father. "The noise might attract someone."

"Here's an old pail," said Leslie. "We can collect water and take it downstairs to use as we need."

Shortly after we regrouped downstairs, Mother began to complain.

"Something's crawling on me!"

"Me, too," I said. "And I don't know what it is."

All night I felt the crawling. I could scarcely sleep.

When daylight came, Father lit the candle for a brief time. I caught one of my visitors as it climbed up my arm and held it to the light. It was a lice, the ultimate humiliation.

"Mother, I think we have lice."

"Oh, no!" Her revulsion matched mine.

"Where did they come from?" I asked.

My eyes fell on the overcoats. "The coats! The soldiers must have had lice."

Soon we were all itching and scratching. To occupy ourselves, we kept a running total of how many of the little beasts we caught. Since lice multiply rapidly, there were plenty to go around.

The week dragged by, and our supply of pickled herring dwindled. I fervently hoped that our mysterious guide would bring us something else when he came again.

"I wish I had a cup of tea," I said one day.

As if by magic, George pulled a crumpled tea bag out of his jacket.

"Don't look so astonished," he said. "I grabbed it when we left the factory. You know I hate to leave anything behind."

"But where will we get boiling water?"

George thought for a minute.

"I have an idea, Mari. Just wait here."

He went upstairs and returned with a broken cup full of water.

"Light the candle," he said. "Tomorrow our guide returns and we get another."

He held the candle under the cup until the china became so hot it scorched his fingers. Slowly the tea began to steep.

"There you are, Mari," he said as he presented me with my wish come true. "I would give safety to you and our child if I could. Since I can't manage that, here's a cup of tea instead."

As we waited for our guide the next day, we were conscious of the escalation of the bombing all around us. For the past few days, the frequency and intensity of the fighting had been obvious.

"It's bombing or shelling from ground forces as well as airplanes," agreed the men. "That can mean only one thing. The Russians have Budapest under siege."

The end was in sight. When Budapest finally fell to the Russians, the Germans and their anti-Semitism would go. We just needed to hang on until it happened. ·

Where was our guide? Another day and night passed, and a third day dawned finding us foodless and worried.

"He's abandoned us," said Father, ever the pessimist. "We must make new plans. We have survived this long, and we will not starve to death in a lousy cellar with liberation so close! One of us must go for help."

We sat in silence, contemplating the possibilities.

"We'll go to Mr. Kapitan," said Father. "He lives nearby, he's a reasonable man, and I'm sure he'll help us." Father sounded more certain of assistance than he actually was. Turning to a Gentile was always risky. Would he be willing to jeopardize his family and himself for us? And would he be able to resist the bounty money we could bring? Father's willingness to risk all on a Gentile acquaintance was an accurate indication of his desperation.

"I have some money to cover any expenses," he said, as much to convince himself as us that the terrible risk was actually minimal.

"Who's Mr. Kapitan?" I whispered to George.

"A business contact of Father's who is the head chef at one of Budapest's best restaurants."

Mother stirred. "I'm the one who should go see him."

"Impossible," said Father and her three sons.

"Paul, you know it must be me," she said to Father. "I'm the one who doesn't look Jewish."

I looked at Mother with her light complexion and gray eyes. She was right.

"I'll put a scarf over my head, and anyone who sees me will think I'm a peasant woman." She quickly knotted her scarf beneath her chin. "See?"

"Why would any sane peasant woman be out walking around during a bombardment?" Father asked.

"I'll go with her," I said. "Anyone who see us will assume there's a problem because of my pregnancy."

Now George's scowl matched Father's.

"Have we an alternative?" asked Mother, presenting her final and strongest argument.

In mid-afternoon she and I set off. Everything looked so bright and spacious after our week cramped in the cellar. It took a while for my eyes to adjust to the glare.

Only a few people were on the street, each hurrying and preoccupied. We blended in well, looking just as worried and nervous as the rest.

When Mr. Kapitan opened his door, he recognized Mother at once.

This was the crucial moment.

"Come in! Come in quickly." He drew us into his warm,

comfortable home and led us to a small sitting room. "Take off your coats. I'll go get my wife."

Mother sat, now completely relaxed. Apparently she trusted this man. I began to relax, too.

When he returned with his wife, Mr. Kapitan spoke to me.

"If you'd like, my wife will prepare a bath for you."

A bath! It had been months since my last bath. I could barely contain my delight as I looked at Mother to see if I should accept.

She nodded.

The bath was extraordinary. Somehow they had an endless supply of hot water. I eased my tired, aching body into the water and just lay there.

He leadeth me beside the still waters. He restoreth my soul.

The troubles of the past few weeks fell away. Even the pickled herring and the lice receded as I enjoyed my luxurious, unbelievable soak.

When Mother and I left the Kapitans, he escorted us to the door.

"Tomorrow at three," he said.

Mother nodded. "We'll be ready."

12

Almost

Precisely at three, Mr. Kapitan drove his horse-drawn wagon to our basement.

I looked at him and got goosebumps all over. "Oh, George, he looks too real!"

He sat on the seat of his wagon dressed in a leather coat. On his arm he wore a swastika. If I hadn't known that we had planned this ourselves, I would not have doubted his authenticity for an instant.

"Come quickly," he called.

We hurried out, and he proceeded to tie us loosely together in the back of the wagon.

It was not hard for us to look despairing as he drove us through town. Too many times we had seen prisoners being driven away in just this manner. The rewards offered for Jews made such activity common.

Mr. Kapitan drove us to our first stop, the Swiss protection house where Mama and Papa were.

"Now," he said.

With hammering hearts George and I quickly loosed ourselves and dashed for the door. We looked back to see the rest of George's family being driven slowly away. We knew they were going to the Swedish protection house where Mother's mother was, but an actual arrest couldn't have looked more chilling.

"Come Mari," said George, taking me by the hand and pulling me into the house. "They'll be all right."

When we burst into Mama and Papa's apartment, we were greeted with tears and joy.

"Oh, Mari," cried Mama. "We were so worried! We had no idea whether you'd reached George or not." She kissed us both again and again. "I'm so glad you're here!"

Papa just hugged us warmly, then contacted his friend and former employee Lajos. Soon George had a Swiss protection letter. We fell so quickly into the old routine that it seemed as if I'd never left. Even the lard and jelly were a welcome change from the pickled herring.

One night there was a furtive knock on the door.

Mr. Hegyi opened it cautiously. The streets were so dangerous at night that anyone who traveled them had to be up to no good.

"Alex! Dezsö, Erzsébet, it's Alex!"

Mama and Papa cried as they hugged their older son. They received no word from him since he had been recalled to forced labor last April. Now suddenly, magically, here he was with his friend Stuli.

Not everyone was as delighted to see Alex and Stuli as we were. They represented two more mouths to feed, two more escapees the Nazis would love to catch to the detriment of those who protected them, and two more people to sleep in the already overcrowded apartment.

Alex and Stuli solved the sleeping problem by sleeping in the bathroom, Alex in the bathtub and Stuli on the floor beside it.

"So tell us, son," said Papa the next day. "How did you escape?"

"Well, Papa, it wasn't so bad this time. I was sent to Jaszbereny here in Hungary, still working in the kitchens like before. When the Arrow Cross began their deportations in October, the Hungarian soldiers in Jaszbereny took all of us Jews and hid us in a large warehouse."

"They did that?" Mama was impressed.

"Of course they couldn't keep us hidden forever," said Stuli. "When they could no longer protect us, they were forced to march us to Budapest for deportation. It came down to them or us."

"As we were marching, I decided to escape," said Alex.

"Just like that?" I said, struck by the calm way he announced such a momentous decision.

"Just like that," he said. "If they shot me in the attempt, so what? I was going to die anyway. It was worth the chance that I might make it, and it was definitely better than dying in some boxcar or gas chamber. When we marched past Kerepesi Cemetery, I made my break."

"I was marching directly behind Alex," said Stuli. "I saw him motion with his head toward the cemetery, and before I knew it, he was over the fence. Without a second thought, I followed him. I couldn't see him, so I crouched behind a tombstone, waiting for the shot that would kill me. It was a great surprise when none came. The men marched on, and I was alone."

I could picture him, squatting, hugging the stone, listening, listening.

"Suddenly a noise startled me and I spun around," he continued. "There was Alex walking out of a mausoleum."

Alex laughed. "I scared him half to death; you should have seen him."

Stuli spread his hands out to us as he tried to explain his feeling. "Just when I thought I was safe, crash, bang, branches break and a gate clangs. He is not a very quiet man."

"Go on," said Mama. "What happened next?"

"We heard that Jews were being hidden in an old textile factory in Angyalföld," said Alex. "So we went there."

"You did? That's where we were. And we never knew you were there, too?" I couldn't believe the coincidence.

Alex shook his head. "We were turned away because there was no more room."

"You can thank God," said George. "It was raided, and we are the only ones that escaped."

Stuli whistled. "So close! Again! I can't believe I'm still alive."

"We hid for a couple of weeks in a bombed house on Vác Utca near Nyugati Rail Terminal," said Alex. "A sympathetic grocer gave us some food. I didn't know where you people were. The ghetto is empty. Finally I went to Frauli's and she told me you were here."

Alex looked at Papa. "Now I have a question for you. Don't you ever get real food? Is it always lard and jelly?"

Food became an obsession. I would lie awake at night, thinking of the butcher shop. I would envision huge piles of meat beside the sausage machine, and I'd fantasize shoveling it into my mouth.

I developed a wild craving for an onion. One night I even called out for one in my sleep. Mama heard me and began to scour our apartment house for an onion.

"Maybe someone has a Gentile friend who has brought one," she said hopefully. There was not one to be found.

My yearning for an onion grew so overwhelming that I even prayed, "Lord, please, send me an onion!"

One day Lajos knocked at our door.

"Frozen cabbage, Mr. Komlos. I hope you can use it. I'm just sorry it's not more."

"Don't worry, Lajos. You have no idea how we appreciate this. You are a faithful friend."

"What will we do with this?" I asked Mama after Lajos had gone.

"We'll cook it."

"Cook it?" said Papa skeptically. "On what? With what?"

"We have matches," said Mama stubbornly. "We'll cook it." And she began to search for some wood.

I held the frozen cabbage. "Thank You, Lord. It's not an onion, but it's close enough."

Mama found two wooden shoe trees discarded in a closet. She took them, the cabbage, and the matches out onto the balcony. Alex joined her, and for an hour they sat in the bitter cold trying to make a fire.

First Alex struck the matches and Mama tried to shield the flickering flame. Then Mama struck the matches and Alex tried to shield them. When the matches were gone, Alex tried to make a fire by rubbing the shoe trees together. They refused to ignite.

We finally gave up and ate the frozen cabbage raw. It didn't matter; it was food.

As the weather grew colder, the soldiers seemed to grow more fierce. Raids on our house increased, though the men were still usually too lazy to come up to the fifth floor. Whey they did reach us, we just lined up as always and let them search.

The difference was that now we feared for Alex and Stuli. Every time the soldiers came, they fled to the roofs, jumping and climbing from house to house to stay ahead of the searching soldiers. Mama couldn't relax until the boys returned following each raid.

We found ourselves vacillating between hope and despair. From our fifth floor vantage point, we could actually see the Russian soldiers advancing through the city. They were our hope. Yet the Nazis still held our section of Pest.

The fact that our fate was not yet in our own hands was chillingly demonstrated to us one day.

Nazis raided the protection house next door, forcing the people to line up in the street. The soldiers marched them all off in the direction of the Danube, two blocks away. Soon we heard the reports of guns. None of the people returned. They had been shot, one by one, and dumped into the river.

One night around 2 A.M. there was a pounding on all the doors in our house.

"Downstairs, everyone. Downstairs."

I clutched George. At this hour there was only one reason for a raid. We were on our way to the Danube.

Armed men herded us to the lower hall where all was confusion. They tried to force us into lines but the large number of us in the confined area defeated them.

Outside voices were shouting, arguing.

Suddenly the front door burst open and in rushed a harried-looking man from the Swiss embassy.

"Return to your rooms," he shouted. "This house is under the protection of the neutral Swiss government. No one will be harmed here."

A soldier, obviously the ranking officer, followed the man inside and grabbed his arm. "You have no right to interfere with us," he shouted at the official.

"No," the official yelled back. "It is *you* who have no right! This is Swiss territory. Now get out!" He pointed at the door.

The officer stood, arms akimbo, legs spread, staring at the official. We watched in fascinated silence as the Nazi blinked first.

"I may not be able to stop your men tonight, Sir," said the official in a steely voice, pressing his advantage, "but tomorrow I shall surely stop you by a visit to your superiors. If you flaunt international law and take these people whom we regard as Swiss neutrals, you will regret it dearly."

The officer stared at the official a moment longer. Then he turned abruptly, calling an order to his soldiers. "Leave them."

As his words echoed through the hall, we sighed in relief. Yet as we returned to our rooms, other words echoed through my mind.

"Thou shalt not be afraid for the terror by night; nor for the arrow that flieth by day; nor for the pestilence that walketh in darkness; nor for the destruction that wasteth at noonday. A thousand shall fall at thy side and ten thousand at thy right hand; but it shall not come nigh thee . . . Because thou hast made the Lord . . . thy habitation."

As I lay down to sleep, I was unafraid. While others were relying on the men from the embassy to keep us safe, I knew Who was really protecting us. Why He should choose to save us when countless others who loved Him just as dearly were dying, I didn't know. I just knew He was our shield.

We passed our first Christmas as Christians in the Swiss protection house, scarcely aware of the day because each flowed with terrible, monotonous sameness into the next.

Of greater significance to us at the time was the fact that George and I moved into the apartment's only bed. I was getting so large that sleeping on the floor was becoming increasingly awkward. We joined Mama and Papa, Mr. and Mrs. Hegyi, and Duci and Imre in the bed. It was a tight squeeze, but it was much more comfortable than the floor.

13

Home!

Nineteen forty-five arrived amid fierce fighting. The Russians under Marshal Rodion Malinovski continued their advance across Budapest.

Looking out our windows on the fifth floor was like viewing a military documentary film. Soldiers ran in and out of doorways and arches. Shouted orders rang through the streets. The shooting was often so intense that watching from the windows was equivalent to taking your life in your hands.

On January 11, the fighting was unusually intense, and as we watched, we were filled with anticipation. We could almost taste the honey-sweetness of liberation.

Suddenly across the square, a lone soldier approached. On his head he wore an unusual hat, a *kuchma*, the fur-lined cap of a Russian soldier.

"They're here!" shouted someone in the room. "Dear God, they're here!"

"We've made it!"

"We're free!"

"We're alive!"

We shouted and hugged and kissed anyone within reach. For us, the war was over.

Of course we couldn't go anywhere yet. One soldier did not make a liberating army. Still we knew his countrymen would follow close behind.

As the lone soldier became a conquering corps, George began to itch to go home.

"All the Fischers will go to the factory. It will be the meeting place. I want to see how they all are and how the factory fared."

It chafed him that it was still too dangerous to be on the streets. The Russians were proving to be a brutal occupying force, pillaging and raping. If we were to meet any soldiers on the street, they would neither know nor care that we had been of the persecuted that they had liberated. A Hungarian was a Hungarian.

We waited another week until George finally thought it safe. This time, as we bade farewell to Mama and Papa, it was not with despair but hope. We were going home, and soon they would, too.

It was a clear cold day as we began our trek to Köbanya and Fischer Textiles. Snow covered the ground as we crossed Varos Liget, a park nearby. From there we moved into a section of the city liberated before ours.

Our expectations of an easy, safe walk were soon dashed. There was much fighting still going on. Often we would start down a street only to withdraw hastily as bullets began to whine by.

"Go two blocks down, and perhaps you'll be able to get through," called a voice from a window above us.

We followed the suggestion and finally found a street we could travel unmolested. Instead of people fighting, we now found frozen corpses and the carcasses of dead horses. Parts of the horses were missing where people had hacked the meat away for food.

I could imagine the stench of death had it been hot weather, and suddenly I could thank God for the cold.

In mid-afternoon I grasped George's arm. "I can't make it any farther without a rest," I said. I tried to smile. "The distance seems to have increased recently."

He nodded. "Mr. Nagy, my father's foreman, lives near here. He'll let us rest there."

Mr. Nagy welcomed us eagerly.

"And your family, George. How are they?"

"Mother and Father and Charles and Leslie were fine in early December. I'm anxious to get home to see how every one else is."

"Tonight, though, you must stay with us," said Mr. Nagy. "Here is your room."

I looked with delight at the huge double bed just for George and me. I could turn over without disrupting the sleep of seven other people.

In spite of our fatigue and the beautiful bed, we didn't rest well. Concern for the family, the factory, and fears about the Russians preyed on us both.

When we left the next morning, Mr. Nagy cautioned us. "Don't be surprised if the factory is severely damaged. With the bombings and the looting there can't be much left."

Apprehension and anticipation are strange companions, and they hounded us as we continued our trip. Three quarters of Budapest was in ruins, and seven of the eight bridges acrosss the Danube had been destroyed. What could we expect in Köbanya?

Suddenly, Fischer Textiles was before us. With relief we saw that there was no major bomb damage. We quickened our pace, anxious to see close up how things were, anxious to see who might be home already.

As we entered the house at the center of the factory complex, a feeling of desolation swept over me. I had hoped for people, love, a welcome. Instead there were only empty buildings full of destruction. Though the physical plant was intact, papers and books were strewn about and anything of value was gone, taken by the soldiers — Hungarian, German, and Russian — who had looted the grounds.

I bent and retrieved a broken picture from the chaos on the floor. It was a photograph of me that I had had set in marble for George, shattered, like our lives, by a soldier we didn't know.

"At least the house and the plant haven't been damaged badly," I said, trying to cheer George up. "Just the windows and the contents."

He nodded. "We'll stay here in spite of the mess. We'll wait for everyone to come home."

That night we slept soundly, surrounded by the familiarity of the factory.

While we waited for the various Fischers to return, I determined to get rid of my head lice once and for all. I knew that if I covered my head with kerosene, the lice would be killed, but petroleum products were extremely difficult to get hold of. Finally one of the Fischers' former maids, Dada, was able to get some kerosene for me.

As Dada poured the substance over my head, I rubbed it in. Oh, how it burned! I just hoped that it wouldn't kill me while it was killing the lice.

When I could stand it no longer, I washed the kerosene from my hair. It took four shampoos before the oily stuff was gone, and I reeked of it for some time, but I didn't care. I no longer itched.

The days passed and slowly the family returned.

The first to arrive were Mother and Father and Charles and Leslie. How warm the house was that night. Soon Leslie's wife Maca returned from Auschwitz.

Then came Ted who had kept himself alive by working as an airplane mechanic. "Knowing how to keep this textile machinery running came in very handy when I had to convince the authorities I should live."

My old school friend and George's sister Martha and her husband Frank Herman returned, happy to throw aside the tension of living as Gentiles on false identity papers, a device they had been able to use successfully for years with the help of some Gentile friends.

George's older sister Rose had lived at the factory with us before George was called up for labor camp. When the factory was no longer a safe place, she and her two children had been hidden by the children's former governess in the country where they masqueraded as peasants. Soon Rose's husband Alex Vita came home as well, having survived his time in a labor camp.

Finally, word was received that George's remaining brother Marcel was safe. He had been in the Ukraine and had retreated to Debrecen, Hungary, where the Russians had liberated him. He didn't reach Köbanya until March. As if to make light of his experiences, he told us, "Truthfully, I spent all my time in the infirmary trying to convince them I was sick."

Miracle of miracle, George's immediate family had all survived the war. I now anxiously awaited word of my brother Jules.

Soon it came. Jules was home with Mama and Papa and Alex at our old home on Conti Street. He had spent the war in a labor force working on a large farming estate in Ercsi in rural Hungary. The owner had taken a special liking to him and had protected him from deportation, hiding him among the local peasants.

I marveled that while thousands of Jews had died in Hungary alone, including forty-eight of my sixty cousins, the Komlos and Fischer nuclear families had survived the war intact. God had kept his promise to me. "A thousand shall fall by thy side, and ten thousand at thy right hand; but it shall not come nigh thee."

Why God had chosen to keep us safe, I didn't know. I could only attribute it to His sovereign keeping power, and I praised Him mightily for His kindness to us.

Soon Fischer Textiles was producing again, only now

the Russians managed things. The family members were once again advisors and laborers in their own plant, as were Hungarians all over the country. We were definitely a conquered country, an occupied nation.

Hungarian life seemed to fascinate the Russians. As a country we were more advanced materially, and the soldiers delighted in taking as their just booty any item they fancied. Watches were especially admired, and people were often stopped on the street and their watches confiscated.

The Russian captain placed in command of our factory was usually a pleasant enough person. Only when he drank heavily was he intolerable. Then we tried to stay out of his way.

One night he became abusively drunk and sent for me. There was only one purpose to the summons, and I knew it only too well. I was just glad George wasn't in our rooms when the message came. I feared the Russian's violence if George tried to protect me, which I knew he'd do.

I went reluctantly, slowly, to the captain's office, not knowing what else I could do, trying to think how I could dissuade him from touching me. I knew my pregnancy would mean nothing to him in his present condition.

When I entered the office, trying not to reveal my inner terror and trembling, the captain staggered toward me. When he said something to me in Russian, I pointed to my enormous belly. By this time I was almost eight months pregnant.

"Baby. Baby soon," I said as I maneuvered to keep as much space and furniture between us as possible.

He didn't appear to understand me, and he lurched in my direction.

Suddenly the office door flew open and George burst into the room. He stepped between me and the captain.

My heart was in my throat. George was not only smaller and slighter; he was unarmed.

The captain started toward us.

Suddenly he stopped, squinting to bring us into focus. George stood his ground, rigid with anger.

The captain snorted and motioned toward the door. Clearly he wanted George to leave.

George started to move, pushing me ahead of him. He wasn't going to leave without taking me along. My legs would scarcely hold me as I walked toward the door. I kept waiting for the captain to grab us or call us back or maybe even shoot us. He did nothing.

Safe in our room, I collapsed in George's arms.

Thank you, Lord. You kept us safe again.

14

My Baby

I t was the end of January. As I lay in bed, I waited for the small thuds to start in my stomach as they did each night when I relaxed. I felt nothing.

I thought back over the day and realized with sudden fear that I could remember no movement all day. I poked at my stomach.

"What are you doing?" George asked.

"Waking the baby," I said lightly. I didn't want to scare him, but I knew the stillness was not good. If there was no movement by tomorrow, I would have to go see Dr. Orban.

The next day I could think of nothing but my baby as George's Uncle Jeno requisitioned a horse from a neighbor's field and drove me and Rose to Dr. Orban's in his old carriage.

Dr. Orban saw me in what remained of the Frigyessy Clinic in Budapest. Only part of the first floor and the basement were usable, and there was no heat in what had once been a modern, seven story hospital.

Rose sat with me following the examination. She already suspected the truth.

"You cannot expect a living child, Mari," said Dr. Orban gently. "I'm sorry."

I felt a great emptiness at his words. It was as if a part of my own life had left me.

"It would be best to wait for the baby to come naturally," the doctor continued. I heard him as from a great distance. "We will wait until February 20. If the baby hasn't come by then, we'll admit you and induce labor."

I was in a daze as Uncle Jeno drove us home. I thought back to that day in the town square when the soldier had sent me home because I looked too far advanced in my pregnancy. I thought of the military policeman who had taken the slim Gabi instead of the ungainly me. And my heart broke. My precious baby who had saved my life would never live.

"I don't understand how you can take this so calmly," Rose said, mistaking my lack of tears for control. I didn't answer.

As soon as George saw me, he knew. He took me to our room to comfort me.

"What do we do?" he asked softly.

"I have to wait for it to come naturally," I choked out before I began to cry. "For maybe twenty days I have to wait!"

George just held me. He knew this child had meant so much to me over the last few months. He knew I had longed to hold this baby in my arms, to love it. And now there would be no infant to cuddle, no little one to cherish.

I struggled with my grief as I waited, not wanting to be bitter at God, but not understanding. Finally on the morning of February 19 I woke with a strange feeling. As the day wore on, and pains jabbed at me with increasing regularity, I knew I was in labor. Uncle Jeno borrowed the horse again and drove George and me to the hospital. Waves of pain washed over me as we jolted through the war-wracked city until I thought I'd drown in their grip.

We were directed to a room in the basement of the once proud clinic. When George opened the door to the room, my heart contracted. Women, all in various stages of labor, all wearing their coats, lined the peeling, gray wall waiting for their time to have their babies.

I took a seat, dazed by pain, watching through slitted eyes as one after another, the suffering women were taken to the delivery room. Beside me a cracked pipe dripped in steady tattoo, and winter's chill, flowing through the broken windows, froze a small lake at my feet. After an eternity of agony, someone put me on a stretcher. It was my turn.

I dimly recognized Dr. Orban standing at the foot of the delivery table. He was wearing his overcoat, too. It was another hour before the baby came.

"A girl." It was a voice from a great distance.

"Can I see her?" I mumbled.

"No, we must perform tests," someone said.

I was devastated. I desperately wanted to see my daughter, to touch her just once, to thank her for my life, but I was too weak to argue.

The next thing I knew, George was beside me, taking my arm. Dr. Orban took my other arm, and together, they half lifted, half dragged me off the table. I had to get up so the next woman could be delivered.

The recovery room was on the first floor, so I had to walk, George helping me, up the stairs. I was put to bed in a room full of other women. I fell into an exhausted sleep, only to be awakened by someone putting ice packs on my breasts to keep my milk from coming in. I felt as though I were being tortured. I tried to push the packs away, but the nurse bound them tightly to me.

When I awoke again, it was morning. The past day seemed more like a nightmare than reality, but I knew it was real by the great leaden feeling in my body. Still the physical pain did not compare with the emptiness I felt in my heart.

Lord, my baby! My daughter. You saved all of us. Could You

*not have spared her too? Yet I trust You, Lord. You know best. I
don't understand and I hurt so badly, but I trust You.*

In the afternoon George came for me. Since the hospital beds were needed by others, I had to go home to recuperate. Alex came with George, bringing a large tricycle, the kind used by meat men for deliveries. The two men lifted me gently into the large basket on the front of the tricycle, and as Alex pedaled, George walked alongside. They took me to the old house on Conti Street where Mama would take care of me. Frauli came, bringing horsemeat she had gotten from a frozen carcass in the street and prepared for me to help build up my strength. I lay back in the comforting cushion of everyone's love.

In two weeks I was feeling strong again physically and George took me back to Köbanya. The trams were finally back in service, so we rode home.

As I became caught up again in the rhythm of life, often my hand would go to my flattened abdomen. I sorely missed my baby's presence. So many nights as I had feared for and prayed for George, the baby had been my comfort.

Lord, I'm trusting, I really am.

Slowly, slowly the wound healed.

15

Defection

"**M**ari, look!"

I took the newspaper from George's outstretched hands, and gasped as I read the headlines.

"FISCHER BROTHERS DEFECT."

"Charles and Marcel," said George. He ran his hand through his hair as he paced the floor in uncharacteristic agitation. "They went on the train to a soccer game in Vienna and never returned."

My head spun with the implications of my brothers-in-law's actions. "You didn't know they planned to do this?" I asked my husband.

George shook his head.

As I read the article, I felt my world was about to collapse. In the three years since the war's end, we had developed a fine and pleasant life, one in which I found much satisfaction.

Lord, does everything have to be turned upside down again? We've worked so hard to establish ourselves.

In the summer of 1945, at about the same time the Russians gave the management of Fischer Textiles back to the family, George and I began to long for a home of our own. With the idea of finding a small apartment for us, I went into Köbánya. As I walked through the shopping area of town, a small, empty store caught my eye. A sign over it read "Poros Studio." As I peered through the dirty windows, excitement leaped inside me.

"George," I said that night. "I didn't see a good apartment today, but I found the perfect photographer's studio for me. If I take my Master's Examination, I can open my own business. It'll help us get on our feet financially."

With George's blessings, I went back to the little shop the next day. This time when I peered in the window, I saw a man.

"Hello," said the young man as I entered. "Can I help you?"

"I'm looking for the owner."

"I guess that's me. My parents used to own the place, but they're gone now." Otto Poros smiled at me and waved his hand vaguely around the room. "I'm not quite sure what to do with it."

"I'm a photographer. Would you consider renting it to me?" I smiled my most charming smile.

He nodded slowly, obviously thinking. "That might work. I have no training in photography, but I speak Russian. My parents were of Russian descent."

"Then we can be partners, sort of," I said excitedly. "You can talk and I can take the pictures."

Otto agreed quickly. "My thoughts exactly."

We set about cleaning up the studio. I found some old supplies and made some sample photographs for the window. In a few days we were open for business.

Our best customers were Russian soldiers who wanted to have their photographs taken to send home to their families. Otto's Russian fluency was invaluable. Equally so were the flour, lard, and coal with which the Russians paid us. Since money was virtually useless, the payment in goods was much appreciated.

George and I found a small efficiency apartment

nearby and set up housekeeping for the first time. When I felt that familiar feeling in my stomach accompanied by morning nausea, I doubted things could get better. George had a job he enjoyed at Fischer Textiles, I had my photography studio, we had a little apartment of our own, even a pet rabbit who reminded me of Frauli's, and we were going to have a baby. I was happy.

One day my cousin Klara came to the studio.

"Mari, look who I found."

Behind Klara stood Peter Schuck, my first boyfriend. We had learned that Peter had claimed conversion during the war in order to get Gentile papers, but we had never heard more.

"Peter!" I gave him a kiss on the cheek. "How well you look! The war was not too hard on you?"

"And how happy you look, Mari. No, the war was not too bad. I spent most of it in a privileged labor camp for converts. At first it was easy jobs and good food. When things began to get bad, I decided it was time to leave. A friend and I escaped and hid in a Swiss protection house."

I couldn't help smiling. How like Peter to reorganize things to his liking, even in war.

"Unfortunately," Peter continued, "we picked a bad house. One night it was emptied and we were all marched to the Danube. They began shooting us, one by one. There was no place to hide, so I just fell over when the shooting came in my direction. I fell into the river and let myself float along with the dead bodies. I almost froze to death in the water, but some peasants saw me move and pulled me out. They hid me until liberation."

"So close, Peter. Like us." I recounted my stories and finished by saying, "But thank God, all George's and my immediate families survived."

"Be careful who you tell that to, Mari," Peter cautioned. "Not many can say such a thing."

I nodded grimly. "I know. But tell me, what are you doing now?"

"Not much. I'm still looking for the right thing."

I laughed. Peter hadn't changed at all. "I've no doubt you'll find just what you want, and that you'll do well at whatever it is."

Shortly after Peter left, we had another visitor. Otto listened to the man, a Russian officer, then turned to me.

"He wants you to come and take a picture of another Russian officer who was killed by a sniper. He's all laid out in his casket, and they want a picture for his family."

"Oh, Otto, I've never photographed a dead man before."

"I don't think you've got any choice, Mari."

Reluctantly I followed the Russian to his car. He drove me to his quarters, took me inside, and introduced me to his compatriots. They were all very gracious. They took me to a room where the dead man lay in a high sided casket. I was amazed at how alive he looked.

I tried to take the picture, but I couldn't get a good angle. I am short and the casket with its high sides was on a table.

I looked around for something to stand on. I saw a chair and pointed to it. They understood immediately and brought it for me. I climbed up.

The chair wobbled, and I fought a wave of nausea. I hate heights, even small ones.

As I focused my camera, a fly lighted on the corpse. I waited for it to move. It wouldn't do to take a picture of a corpse with a fly on it, especially not the corpse of an officer.

The fly left the body and flew to me. As it landed on my hand, I cringed. My nausea increased at the idea of the insect coming from the dead man to me. It was all I could do not to faint right into the coffin.

As part of our new life of independence, George and I went to Bible study groups where we enjoyed fellowship with Jewish and Gentile Christians alike. My old English tutor Mary Hajos still taught one of these studies though she had given up her English tutoring and become involved in an orphanage, The Good Shepherd Home. I reveled at being under her instruction again.

One of the members of our study was Chuck Graham, an American stationed in Hungary as part of the token United States occupation force. We were very much in awe of Americans, and we marveled that we knew one personally and could claim him as a brother in Christ.

In November, 1945, free, secret ballot elections were held in Hungary for the first time in many years. A coalition government was elected with the Smallholders Party winning 59 percent of the vote. The Communists won only 17 percent. In January, 1946, a republican constitution was adopted. We were pleased to be part of a free, independent Hungary.

As the birth of our baby drew near, George and I moved to a larger apartment with three bedrooms and a maid's room. The only war damage was a hole in the floor which we quickly repaired. I moved the photography studio to the third bedroom and waited anxiously for May.

On May 27, 1946, John Jules Fischer was born. Everything went well this time, and I couldn't wait to cradle my baby. Before he was washed, as he lay on the delivery table, I reached down to touch him. I was a mother at last.

We decided to dedicate John to the Lord at the small evangelical church we attended. Knowing that George's family was still upset at our Christianity, we didn't invite them, but we did invite Mama and Papa and Alex and Jules. Since John carried Jules' name and since both my brothers were asked to be the baby's godparents, they both came to the service. Mama and Papa chose to come only to our apartment afterwards for refreshments. While they were careful not to show any resentment because we no longer attended synagogue, they were disappointed that their first grandson was being dedicated in our new faith.

Near the end of 1946, Mary Hajos decided to visit the United States to raise money for her Good Shepherd Home. We all shared her excitement for to us the United States was a country of greatness and wealth.

"I'd like to visit there some day," I told George.

He grinned. "So would I, but don't hold your breath."

Through 1947, our life continued in its pleasant pattern, and I was happy. Even the signs of the Russian military occupation were becoming less, though the Communists under Mátyás Rákosi were gaining more and more political power. Their weapons for gaining their control were terror and blackmail. In the 1947 elections the Communists took 22 percent of the popular vote, but in 1948, thanks to Rákosi's machinations, they were able to form a wholly Communist government.

With Communist control came the nationalization of industry. Though only major industries were affected at the start, moderate-sized businessmen like Father and small businessmen like Papa became anxious. How far would the nationalization extend?

It was April 16, Good Friday, 1948, when the swift sword of nationalization struck us.

Father was in Switzerland at the time, buying new machinery for the mills when, without any notice, Fischer Textiles was seized.

Mother and all those living on the factory grounds had to vacate their homes immediately, taking nothing with them and receiving no compensation whatsoever.

Father, from his vantage point in Switzerland, understood the situation in Hungary all too well. He had lived under a government that had stripped him of his dignity and business once before, and he would not subject himself to it again. He chose to remain in Switzerland.

The thought of joining Father did not occur to us. Our lives were settled. George could continue to work at the factory, little John was doing well as he waited for the imminent arrival of a sibling, and I had my photography.

Then, two weeks after the mill was seized, came the bombshell of the defection of Charles and Marcel.

"It's one thing for Father to stay in Switzerland since he was already there. It's quite another thing for my brothers to scheme to join him illegally," George said as he frowned in thought. "The question is, how does this affect us?"

"Look at this, George," I said as I read the newspaper article with dreadful fascination. "The way the article calls all you Fischers capitalists, you'd think owning your own business was a crime. I guess it is to them. And it says you are all to be considered enemies of the state! You're not to be employed, and you're to be arrested if found! Oh, George, it's so ridiculous! Can they really arrest you?" Disbelief held my fear in check. The whole situation was too fantastic to be true.

"Who's to stop them?" he asked. "They have the power now."

I hugged John, now almost two, to try and calm myself. I was sure I knew what George was going to say.

"I'm going to have to leave Hungary, too, Mari. Immediately, I don't have any choice."

I nodded, knowing he was right. "But what about me and John? And the baby? It's due in six weeks."

"I don't know yet. I have to think."

That night George sneaked out of the apartment, taking care that the building supervisor, Mr. Peros, a Communist sympathizer, didn't see him. When he returned several hours later, he had already made arrangements for his escape.

"Mother knows a Russian chauffeur who drives a Red Cross ambulance part time. He has agreed to hide Mother, Ted and me in the back of his ambulance tomorrow night and drive us to Vienna — for a sum of money, of course."

My stomach churned and the blood roared in my ears. Tomorrow night!

George put his arms around me.

"We have no option, Mari. You know I don't want to leave you and John, especially with the baby so near. You also know you couldn't travel now. If I were to wait until the baby were born, it might be too late. With Mr. Peros around, I have no illusions about my safety."

"I know," I said through my tears. "I understand, really I do. You have to go and immediately. But what about me and the children?"

"After the baby's born and you're feeling well again, the driver has agreed to bring you and the children out. Until then, you'll have to let people think that I'm in the country looking for work now that I can't hold a job here in Budapest."

Much too soon, I said goodbye to George, once again watching my husband walk into unknown dangers.

Lord, take care of him!

Time passed with agonizing slowness after George left. Each day seemed longer than the last. The apartment was too empty, but much as I hated its desolation, I hated to leave it because of Mr. Peros.

"Ah, Mrs. Fischer," he'd say as he waylaid me at the door. "How's your husband today?"

"We're all fine, Mr. Peros. George is still in the country looking for work."

I felt no guilt about misleading the man. George was in the country, Austria, looking for work. I was surprised that my answer satisfied our apartment superintendent, but I didn't know how long I could continue to deceive him. I am not a good liar.

June came, and as the baby's birth drew nearer, I began to worry about the plan to spirit me and children out of Hungary. We would have to drug the children to ensure their silence, and the thought of doing that to babies upset me. There would be so little room for error. *Lord, hold me. I feel so unsteady!*

The night of June 8, I went into labor, and in the afternoon of the following day the baby was born, a beautiful girl we had decided to name Andrea before George left. Much as I welcomed Andrea, I had feared my confinement for I was scared that I would mention our escape plans while under the influence of the pain-dulling drugs.

Once the delivery was behind me, and I hadn't revealed our plans inadvertantly, my daughter was a great joy. She lay in her crib at the foot of my hospital bed, and if it hadn't been for George's absence and the curiosity it aroused, I would have been content.

The day after Andrea's birth, Mama and Papa brought John to the hospital to see his new sister. He was delighted to meet someone smaller than he, and he demanded the right to kiss her. Mama lifted him over the side of the crib, and he bent down and kissed the baby's feet. Tears sprang to my eyes at the beautiful picture they made.

When I went home, Mama came every day to help me with the children. I was anxious to recuperate completely so I could join George. It bothered me that I wasn't bouncing back as quickly as I felt I should. Where was the resilience I had had under stress during the war?

Lord, I'm too rocky. Keep me firm on the Rock!

The consequences of leaving Hungary began to weigh heavily on me. As I watched Mama with John and Andrea, I wanted to cry. What would life be for her and Papa without their grandchildren, without me? What would life be for me without her and Papa?

Physically, I soon felt fine, but emotionally I was drained.My feelings were very near the surface, and I felt I wasn't quite in control. Mr. Peros did nothing to help.

"Ah, Mrs. Fischer," he'd say. "Such a beautiful baby. Isn't it a shame Mr. Fischer hasn't been able to get home even once to see her?" And he'd stare at me suspiciously.

Under his constant, prying eye, I found it increasingly difficult to keep up the fiction of George's job hunt in the country. I knew I had to leave — and quickly.

I made contact with the Russian ambulance driver and set the time for our trip to Vienna. I bought the medicine to drug the children. I packed my overnight case with the few things I could take.

Mama came over for what we both knew would be the last time. She was quiet and sad; the children, sensing something was about to happen, were cranky and fussy; and I felt ready to fragment into a multitude of quivering pieces.

Suddenly I began to cry.

"Shush, Mari," Mama said. "It'll be all right."

"I know," I sobbed. "I know." I tried to stop my tears, but the more I tried, the harder I cried.

Mama took me in her arms. "Come on, dear. Calm yourself. You're upsetting the babies."

"I know," I said, clinging to her. My sobbing neared hysteria, and Mama grew concerned.

"I'm going to call the doctor."

"No!" I shouted. "I can't tell anyone about our escape plans." And I cried even harder.

Mama sat me down and went to the phone. I watched her, feeling helpless and scared as tears streamed down my face.

In a few minutes Dr. Szabo was there. He took one look at me and said, "Mari, you can't go anywhere in your condition."

"But George is waiting for me," I sobbed.

"You'll just have to let him know you're not coming tonight. What good would it do for you to drug the children to silence if you can't control your own tears? You'd most certainly be found out. Where can George be reached?"

I gave him the address.

"Good. It's settled then. No trips tonight or for some time. You need several weeks of rest before you can go anywhere. Now I'm going to give you something to help you sleep."

I lay back and cried until I finally drifted off.

16

The Hand of God

I awakened to darkness, my heart racing with terror.

"George!"

"Shush, Mari." It was Mama. "It's all right. I'm here." At the sound of her voice, the vise of fear relaxed and my nightmare receded.

"Oh, Mama, I had such a terrible dream!" I took a deep breath to quiet myself. "George came to meet me and the children as we'd planned, but when the ambulance pulled up, the driver grabbed him and sped away." I shuddered. "It was so vivid! We have to get word to George that we aren't coming."

I began to climb out of bed.

"Papa's already called George," said Mama as she tried to keep me lying down.

"Did he actually talk to him? Are you certain he talked to George?"

"Yes, I'm certain. Everything has been taken care of. George's in no danger. Now you must go back to sleep."

I allowed her to cover me, and I fell into a restless sleep. The next time I awoke, it was morning. I could hear Mama and Papa talking in the kitchen.

"What did you tell George?" Mama asked.

"I told him Mari was ill and could not come. He asked how long it would be before she was well enough to travel."

"What did you say?"

"I told him that if he wanted to see her again, he'd better come back here where he belonged."

"Oh, Dezső, you didn't!"

"I did."

"You shouldn't have and you know it. If they feel they must leave Hungary, we have to let them go."

Papa muttered something I couldn't understand. Poor Papa.

"Do you think I want them to leave?" Mama asked, her voice harsh. "But we can't make a decision like this for them. What did George say?"

"He'd find some way back."

My heart grasped those words and held them tightly. George was coming back to me. Tears sprang to my eyes again, but it didn't matter. The pressure of the last months was gone. George was coming home.

Thank you, Lord. Just help him not to be angry with me.

A few days later George was home. A slim, dark man, short of stature and narrow of shoulders and hips, my husband did not look the stuff of which heroes are made. But physical appearances can be deceiving; I knew they could mask the courage of a lion. I reveled in the security of his presence, his arms about me.

"How did you get back?" I asked.

"The same way I got out," he said. "The driver thought I was crazy, but as long as he got paid, he was willing to reverse the procedure."

"You don't know how glad I am to have you back!" I said.

"And I'm glad to see you," he said quietly.

"But you're upset."

"Not with you, Mari. With the circumstances. I'm still a capitalist in a Communist country, essentially a fugitive. I can't leave the apartment without being in grave danger.

And I can't let Mr. Peros know I'm here or we'll be under constant surveillance with no chance ever to escape."

Suddenly the selflessness of George's actions struck me. He had sacrificed his freedom to return to me. Such behavior spoke with an eloquence beyond words, and his love for me was matched only by my devotion to him.

With George home, my health improved quickly. When I was able to be up and around, we decided to check the different embassies to ascertain our chances of leaving the country legally. It would be so much safer for the children.

It was not easy to leave a Communist country, and I soon found out the truth of this fact. Each time I went out for food or some other necessity, I visited an embassy. No one could give me hope.

Then an official at the Swiss embassy recommended I try the Paraguayan embassy. There, visas were being issued to anyone willing to come to that South American country. Being small and backward, Paraguay valued and was seeking anyone who could bring a technical skill to the country.

When I arrived at the embassy, I found that many others had heard the same story. There would be much competition for the visas, these tickets to life. I got all the necessary forms and took them home to George.

The very next day, I returned the completed forms. Attached to them was an envelope containing money.

"There are so many applying for these visas," said George. "This will help insure that they consider us carefully."

It was a difficult three days as we waited for our application to be processed. During that time we prayed earnestly for God's intervention on our behalf. Finally I returned to the embassy.

"Fischer," I said to the official when it was my turn. I

watched nervously as he went through his files in slow motion.

"Ah, here it is," he said. "Everything seems to be in order." He handed me our papers, a big ACCEPTED stamped across them. The envelope and money were gone.

"You have your visas," said the official. "Now you must get your Hungarian passports. I warn you that it may be very difficult."

"Thank you," I said, grinning widely. His warning didn't worry me. Surely the Lord who had gotten us our visas to enter Paraguay would get us our passports to leave Hungary.

I went to the passport office, an impressive building manned by Hungarian Communists who would not be sympathetic with the plight of a capitalist like me. It was important to the Communists not to let the young and the educated leave our country. They — and that included us — were too valuable to the State.

When I showed my visa and asked for the passport office, I was directed to Room 27. I walked down the hall, clutching my papers in my hand. At Room 27, I knocked nervously on the door.

"Come in."

An official sat behind an enormous desk working on some papers.

"Yes?" he said and looked up.

My heart skipped a beat. It was Peter Schuck. For a moment neither of us spoke.

Finally he said carefully, "May I help you?"

"I would like to apply for passports for my husband and me. We have visas for Paraguay." I handed him the papers.

"We do not issue many passports," he said formally, "but we will consider your application. Come back in a few days."

I nodded and left, somewhat dazed. How had Peter ever gotten such a high Communist position? Had he really become a Communist? Somehow I doubted it. Peter had a way of convincing people. I was certain that God was going to use Peter to get us our passports.

"And we know that all things work together for good to them that love God, to them who are the called according to His purpose."

In three days I returned to the passport office.

"I'm afraid there's been a delay," said Peter. He looked genuinely concerned. "Come back in a few days."

My face must have shown my fear and consternation. He leaned close and said very softly, "I'm trying to push this through." I smiled my appreciation.

When I reached our apartment building, I found Mr. Peros waiting for me.

"You're keeping very busy these days, aren't you, Mrs. Fischer?" He glared at me, suspicion peering out of his narrowed eyes.

I ignored him and hurried to the apartment where I waited four more days before going to see Peter again.

"I'm here about the Fischer passport," I said as I entered Room 27 for what I hoped would be the last time.

He looked up quickly and smiled. "I think that has been approved," he said officially.

My heart reeled with excitement as he handed me the passports. We were free! I squeezed his hand.

"Thank you," I breathed.

When I handed George the papers, he read through them a number of times. It was as if he couldn't believe they were real. Finally he grinned triumphantly and re-laxed for the first time since his return.

17

Budapest to Ellis Island

We left Hungary at 2 o'clock on Friday, November 1, 1948. As of this date, George had spent four months hiding in our apartment. Even when we left for the train station we were careful not to let Mr. Peros see George. We wanted no last minute trouble.

The months of preparation for our journey had been hard on Mama and Papa.

"How do you know you'll like Paraguay?" Papa often asked.

"We don't," I answered. "But it has to be better than here."

"How can you take the babies to a place you know so little about?"

"I have no choice, so I must trust them to God. He'll protect them."

"George," Papa said, "I still have my meat market. Work for me."

"Thanks, but you know I can't. I'd be found out sooner or later. We must go."

Finally we stood on the platform waiting for our train to Vienna, Austria, for the first leg of our journey.

Some of our Christian friends had come to see us off, though they had officially bid us godspeed at Wednesday night's Bible study. I had been blessed by their prayers for

us and the verse they had selected for our encourage-
ment.

"And we know that all things work together for good to
them that love God, to them who are the called according
to his purpose. (Rom. 8:28)"

God had previously used that verse to comfort me, and
their choice of it was further proof of His promise to go
before us. Our Christian friends also gave us a letter of
recommendation to the Christian brothers we hoped to
meet in Paraguay.

Also standing on the train platform to see us off were
Frauli and Leo, Alex and his wife Agnes, and Jules and
his wife Cornelia.

Surrounded by our friends and family, yet looking
forlorn and lonely were Mama and Papa.

"George," pleaded Papa one last time, "wait a little
longer. Maybe things will get better."

George shook his head. "We can't wait."

The conductor gave the call for boarding.

My heart began to pound and my throat felt so thick I
could hardly swallow. The final goodbyes. I prayed I
wouldn't cry.

I kissed my brothers and sisters-in-law, then Frauli,
then Mama, and lastly Papa. He stood tall above me. Even
now with two children of my own, I felt like a child beside
him, my tower of strength.

Suddenly he lay his head on my shoulder and wept.

"Dear Papa, I love you." I tried to comfort him, but I
was afraid to say more lest I too begin to cry.

George took John and I took Andrea in her wicker
basket. We found our seats just as the train began to
move. We watched our loved ones from the window until
they disappeared from view. Then my tears began and I
let them flow all the way to Vienna.

Mother and Father met our train in Vienna and let us

stay with them until we could find a place of our own. We knew it would be some time before we could get steamship tickets to Paraguay because transportation was still chaotic even three years after the war. Finally we found a room in the Hotel Gablerbrau in Salzburg where we could live until we left Europe.

Things were cramped with the four of us in the one room. I had to do our laundry in the room's sink. Still we were free. We could go for walks around beautiful Salzburg whenever we pleased without fear. When Mother and Father came to Salzburg to be near us, my feeling of loss for my family was somewhat alleviated.

For over two months George sought tickets for our trip across the Atlantic. Finally he secured passage aboard the *SS America*, due to sail for New York City January 20, 1949.

"There's only one problem," he said as he showed me the tickets. "We have to be in separate cabins. You and the children will have one and I'll be next door with another man. It was that or wait who knows how long."

"It's all right," I said. "We'll manage. It's only a matter of days. And since the *America* sails to New York City, we'll get to see a little bit of the United States on our Visitor's Visas."

I repacked our belongings, and five days before our sailing date we boarded a train for Paris via Zurich, Switzerland. Mother and Father came to see us off.

"George," said Father just before we boarded our train, "this is for you." He handed George an envelope. "When I was in Switzerland buying machinery last spring, I had a large sum of money with me to pay for the purchase. When the factory was nationalized, of course I didn't complete my dealings. Instead I divided the money into equal shares for you and your brothers. Here is your portion. Use it to get established in Paraguay."

We hugged Mother and Father and climbed aboard.

If it weren't for the pain of the goodbyes and the uncertainty of ever seeing our families again, I thought, I could enjoy this trip.

We spent three days in Paris before going to LeHavre, France and the SS *America*. I was thrilled by the beauty of the ship, especially when we cabin class people were allowed to tour the first class facilities before we sailed.

"Oh, George, how grand!"

But I was still unprepared for the dazzle and delights of the dining room. Pushing aside the queasy feeling I was experiencing from the ship's motion, I followed George upstairs for dinner.

The dining room looked like a grand ballroom. Chandeliers rained light on us as we took our seats at a table set with linens, silver, and crystal. John was entranced at the glories of the magnificient room and I was entranced with the menu. Column after column of every imaginable food was offered, foods that in recent years I'd only dreamed about. Roast goose, veal cutlet, prime rib. Only short days ago I'd been standing in long lines at shops, my ration cards in my hand, John along to hopefully touch the shopkeeper's heartstrings so he'd be moved to give us a bit extra. Now I could eat any quantity of anything I wanted.

Ignoring the increasing swaying of the chandeliers and discomfort in my stomach, I ordered something from each column on the menu. I kept swallowing as I waited for my appetizer.

No sooner had the waiter placed the fresh fruit cup before me than I bolted. There was no time for explanations. I reached my cabin just in time to be violently sick.

As I lay moaning on my bunk, trying not to see the spinning of the room, George appeared with John.

"What's happening?" I managed to ask.

"We're in a storm with very rough seas," he said as he braced himself against the walls. Suddenly he dashed for his room.

As the ship pitched and bucked, John played contentedly, but Andrea began to complain. She was hungry.

I made an attempt to get up, but the lurching of the ship threw me back. Finally I made it to my feet, but I was afraid to lift the baby from her basket for fear I'd drop her. I pulled the basket next to my bunk, and bracing myself, I lifted her to the bunk and let her nurse. She had difficulty getting enough to satisfy her.

The next day both the ship and I were just as rocky, and I had to call the ship's nurse on the phone. When she finally came, I told her I couldn't nurse the baby properly because I was so sick.

She disappeared to return soon with some small jars and a little spoon. She pointed to the jars and then Andrea. I had never heard of feeding a baby from a jar before but since there was a picture of a baby on the label, this was obviously what I was supposed to do. The nurse left, and I opened one of the jars. Andrea had no trouble with the new way of eating and seemed to enjoy the taste of the food. She ate the whole jar full.

George, feeling about as sick as I, stumbled over to visit us.

"I've got to stay here for a while," he said. "My cabin mate smokes wretched cigars, and their stench is making me even sicker than the storm.

"George, we've got to find someone to care for John."

He stumbled off to find the nurse. When he returned, he said someone would be along soon to take John to the nursery where he would be watched over attentively.

"They're terribly busy upstairs," he said. "75 percent of the passengers are seasick because of these wretchedly severe seas, and there's no break in the weather in sight."

I groaned, shutting my eyes to block out the constant motion. I opened them immediately. I couldn't decide which was worse, watching everything sway or feeling it sway.

Andrea had begun to cry. I picked her up and tried to comfort her, but she kicked and cried and would not be soothed.

"Not now, honey. Don't you get sick, too. Not now, please."

In answer, she screwed her face up tighter, drew up her little legs and screamed. I guessed it was the baby food making her unaccustomed system gaseous. I tried to nurse her.

When the ship's nurse came for John, she asked if the baby had eaten. I showed her the empty jar. She read the label and blanched. Not knowing that much English, I had been unable to read the word "prunes." Poor Andrea cried all day.

The third day of our journey was even worse than the two previous ones. Now the rolling was so severe that the suitcases fell out of their racks. I was afraid I would die and afraid I wouldn't.

A steward came to our door. "You must get some fresh air. Let me help you to a deck chair."

After he got us settled, he said, "Whatever you do, don't look down. Keep your eyes on the horizon. Don't look down. Now I'll get you some broth."

I looked at the raging sea, an endless expanse of angry, churning foam-flecked gray, and felt as buffeted as it looked. When my broth came, I sipped it carefully. To my relief, it stayed down.

The next day, the seas were calmer and we were able to handle broth and toast. By day six, January 25, we were feeling almost normal. The excitement of docking in

New York City, the United States of America, gripped us. Our Visitor's Visas would allow us to sight-see until our connecting ship was ready for the rest of the trip.

Immigration officials boarded the ship after we docked, and we gladly showed them our papers. After they examined them, the men began to talk to us. I knew they must be speaking English, but it sounded nothing like what I had learned from Mary Hajos.

Gradually we began to understand that there was a problem with our papers, though the officials didn't explain what. They just told us to follow them. I looked anxiously at George. What could possible have gone wrong?

We collected our belongings and followed the immigration officials off the ship and into a car. They drove onto a ferry which took us to a small island. A sign where we docked read "Ellis Island Detention Camp."

We sat, stunned, unable to believe what was happening, unable to understand why.

We were shown to a room that was comfortable enough, though there were bars on the windows.

"What's wrong?" I asked on the verge of tears. "Are we prisoners?"

George had no more idea than I.

Food was brought to us, but no explanation of our confinement was given. We did the only thing we could do. We knelt in prayer. Surely the Lord who had brought us this far would take care of us now.

As darkness fell, I went to our window and peered out between the bars. There, not far away, bathed in lights, stood the Statue of Liberty, that great American symbol of freedom.

18

An Alien in America

Darkness clamped down on Ellis Island and I struggled against feelings as black as the night outside our barred window. America, land of the free, home of the brave. If only there was someone we could turn to.

Suddenly I remembered a piece of paper Mary Hajos had given me before we left Hungary. I fumbled through our things looking for it.

"Mari, what are you doing?" George asked.

"Remember the name Mary gave us before we left, those people she stayed with while she was here raising money for her Good Shepherd Home? Maybe they can help us. Here! I've found it." I spread out the paper on the bed. "Mr. and Mrs. Hector Sinzheimer. They're Hebrew Christians as we are and they live in some place called Mt. Airy near Philadelphia. Is that near here?"

"How should I know?" said George. "But tomorrow we'll contact them. Maybe they can at least find out what's wrong."

I fell asleep thanking the Lord for Mary's slip of paper, given me as a last minute thought that neither of us had expected to come to anything.

"Just in case," she'd said as she pressed the scrap into my hand.

The next day George sent a telegram to Mr. Sinzheimer and we sat back to wait. Another day passed before there was any response, and it was unexpected.

"You have a visitor," said the official as he opened the door for an American lady.

"I'm Ann Goldman," she said. "Are you all right?"

We nodded.

"Mr. Sinzheimer asked me to come see you. He and Mrs. Sinzheimer want you to come and stay at their home as soon as you can leave here."

"But how do we make such arrangements?" asked an overwhelmed George.

"I've learned that you'll have a hearing this afternoon to tell you about your difficulties. I'll be back after it's over, when you know more. Don't worry. Everything will be fine."

Mrs. Goldman left, and George and I stared at each other, dumbfounded. Not only had the Sinzheimers come to our aid; they had sent a friend and they were willing to take us into their home. How good the Lord was.

In the afternoon at our hearing, we finally learned what the problem was. While we had been riding out the storm at sea, Paraguay had been going through a political storm. When the *coup d'etat* was over, the new government had canceled all visas issued in Europe by the old government. We were literally people without a country.

"What about our Visitor's Visas issued by this country?" we asked the immigration people.

"To enter the United States on a Visitor's Visa, you must have a secured departure date," they told us. "You no longer have one."

"We no longer have anything," said George.

After the hearing we were returned to our rooms while the immigration authorities debated what to do with us.

The next day at another hearing, we were told that if

we could post $1000 bond, we would be allowed to stay in the United States for four months on our Visitor's Visas. During this time it was our responsibility to acquire visas to another country.

Since we could post the bond, thanks to Father's farewell gift, we agreed.

Later that day, Mrs. Goldman came for us. We were finally going to see America, and in spite of our rocky introduction, I fully expected to love this country and its streets of gold.

While the golden streets were noticeably missing, I wasn't disappointed. In fact I was amazed, especially at the size of everything.

"I'm going to put you on the train to Philadelphia," said Mrs. Goldman. "But first let's get something to eat."

She took us to a large restaurant called Horn and Hardart's. What an amazing place! I pushed my tray down a counter, and watched bemused as little windows popped open and food appeared. The last door opened to reveal red stuff that wiggled. It was Jello, something I had never seen before.

When Mrs. Goldman left us at the train, she assured us that Mrs. Sinzheimer would be waiting for us in Philadelphia. The trip passed quickly in spite of our nervousness as, fascinated, we watched New Jersey rush by.

As soon as we stepped off the train in Philadelphia, a short round woman about fifty with a big smile, rosy cheeks, and warm friendly eyes came toward us with open arms.

"Hello, Marianne and George. I'm Olive Sinzheimer and we're so glad to have you with us." She looked at the children in surprise. "And who have we here?"

In our telegram to the Sinzheimer's and in a letter Mary had written them after we left Budapest, and before we arrived in America, no one had thought to mention John and Andrea. The oversight presented no problem, for the children were as welcome as we.

Soon we were settled in the guest room of the Sinzheimers' large Mt. Airy home, complete with cribs quickly borrowed from friends.

That evening when Mr. Sinzheimer came home, we had a wonderful dinner. Our hosts listened patiently to our fumbling English as we explained our situation. They urged us to stay with them while we sought our new visas.

We were only too happy to accept their hospitality, and I wrote Mama and Papa all about our new American friends.

John quickly accepted Mrs. Sinzheimer as another grandmother, and she taught him to call her Granny. Soon we were all calling her Granny and Mr. Sinzheimer became *Bacsi*, the Hungarian word for uncle.

I was fascinated by the new things I saw in America, and Granny enjoyed teaching us all the mysteries of her country.

"Come. We'll go shopping," she said.

George, the children, and I went along eagerly.

"This is called a supermarket, and we do most of our shopping here," Granny explained. "Marianne, why don't you put the baby in the shopping cart?"

I looked extremely puzzled, and she showed me the clever manner in which the front of the cart folded down to make a seat for Andrea. We wheeled her around the store as John clung to the back of the cart and Granny filled it.

The sheer number of items available was overwhelming, but what amazed me most was the frozen food, an innovation just coming into its own and something I'd never seen before.

As we put the groceries, stored in crisp brown paper

bags instead of wicker baskets carried from home, in the trunk, it suddenly struck me. We wouldn't have to shop each day as we did in Hungary. Everything would be kept fresh in the large refrigerator in Granny's kitchen.

"Let's stop at the bakery before we go home," Granny said. "You can pick out the dessert."

A fat, circular, dough-topped dish in the display case caught my eye.

"What is that?"

"An apple pie, Marianne, a very traditional American dish."

"What's inside the pastry?"

"Fruit. Apples, all cut up and baked."

I was fascinated. I had never heard of doing such a thing to fruit, but one taste convinced me that it was a good idea.

In Hungary we had always had a maid and a nurse for the children, as had everyone else. I had never had to look after my home or my children. I quickly learned that in America only the rich have domestic help, and I was expected to know how to care for my children and how to do housework.

When Granny discovered my ignorance, she lovingly taught me all the things I needed to know. She taught me how to cook American dishes and how to iron a shirt on that ingenious implement, an ironing board. She taught me to dust and to wash dishes with fragrant liquid detergent. She taught me how to bathe my children, and I especially enjoyed bathing Andrea in Granny's kitchen sink.

The first Saturday we stayed with Granny and Bacsi, they took us to a meeting of Messianic believers at Philadelphia College of the Bible. I was sitting between George and Granny listening to these people sharing what the Lord had done for them when Granny prodded my arm.

"Give your testimony," she whispered.

I looked at her, puzzled. What did "testimony" mean?

"Tell what the Lord has done for you," she encouraged. "God will fill your mouth."

I was struck by the thought that God would give me the words I needed. I rose, said a sentence or two, and sat quickly, finished. But I never finished claiming the promise that God would fill my mouth as I struggled to share His graciousness in a new language.

The Sinzheimers also took us to church with them. To prevent my becoming too confused by the language barrier, Bacsi bought me a Hungarian Bible. When the pastor read in English, I would follow in Hungarian. I liked the irony of having studied an English Bible in Hungary and now using a Hungarian Bible in America.

American Sunday School was a totally new concept to us. I often had to sit with John or Andrea in their classes as they got over feeling strange, and I loved the Bible stories being taught to the children at their levels.

In July we went to our first Sunday School picnic. The games and prizes for the children, the food, the fun, and the fellowship made it a day we would never forget.

Numerous little cultural differences between the Sinzheimers and us cropped up. One became obvious our first Sunday in their home. As we prepared to leave for church, I noticed Granny put on a hat.

"Why do you wear a hat like that?" I asked, thinking it not very practical.

"It is our custom here, our headcovering." She held one out to me. "Here. You wear this one."

I did though I thought it unnecessary.

At breakfast each morning Granny offered John a piece of toast.

"Toasted bread is for sick people," he'd say. "I want real bread."

But American white bread was an offense to his Hungarian taste buds and their craving for a coarser, darker bread much like Jewish rye. Gradually he learned to endure white bread.

Around his neck John wore a gold chain from which hung a gold medallion depicting Raphael's little praying angel.

"Why does John wear that necklace?" Granny asked. "In America boys do not wear jewelry." They especially didn't in her conservative church circles.

"In Hungary all little boys wear such a necklace. It is a gift from their grandparents, a keepsake."

"It looks strange."

"Then we will take it off." And we did.

"How about Andrea's and your pierced ears and earrings? Does everyone have them, too?"

I nodded. "Her ears were pierced by our doctor when she was three days old and still in the hospital. The earrings are a gift from my mother as mine are from my mother's mother."

She nodded satisfied, and Andrea kept wearing her earrings.

These little differences never became problems because between us the love we shared in Christ overcame them. One of us always accommodated the other.

George practiced his English by reading the newspapers each day and by studying an English engineering manual. He spent much time in correspondence with embassies as we tried to find new visas.

The four months of our Visitor's Visas passed with no success, so we applied for and were granted a four month's extension.

We couldn't keep imposing on Granny and Bacsi's hospitality indefinitely, so in June we moved from their lovely home to a furnished house nearby. The owner of our new home was a chef who worked summers at the

New Jersey shore. He rented his home in Philadelphia from June until the middle of September for a modest fee. Surely we would be leaving the United States before he returned at summer's end to reclaim his home.

Daily Granny came to see us, and always she brought something. As a result the drain on our limited resources was minimal. Because we were on a Visitor's Visa, George was forbidden to work.

My ability as a meat packer trained under Papa helped me now. While meat was very expensive, I knew it was good for us and wanted to serve it each day. I also knew that while two-day old meat didn't look too nice and might actually feel slimy, it was still edible if cleaned up with a vinegar and water solution. Therefore I bought the older, cheaper meats and we were able to eat well on little.

I wrote regularly to Mama and Papa about Granny and Bacsi's kindnesses to us, and soon the Sinzheimers received a letter from Papa expressing his gratitude.

Since the letter was written in English and Papa knew no English, I realized he had gone to the one person he knew in Budapest who could help him, Mary Hajos. Knowing Mary, I was certain that Papa had heard again the claims of the Messiah. He also had seen the love of Christ at work on our behalf in Granny and Bacsi, and I knew he had to be moved. I beseeched God that He would open Papa's understanding and that Papa would recognize Jesus as his Messiah.

Suddenly it was September, we had no new visas, and the chef wanted to return to his home. We moved again, this time to a row home with three small bedrooms and a kitchen so tiny that I had to put a cutting board over the sink to have work space.

We had met a Messianic believer named Dave Robinson at some meetings for refugees that Granny and Bacsi had taken us to. Dave had become a friend, and when we moved into our row home, he signed a note for us on the second-hand furniture we bought, guaranteeing its payment. What wonderful American friends God was providing for us.

One night as I finished putting the children to bed, there was a knock at our door. My heart lurched. Memories of nighttime raids gripped me. I watched fearfully as George opened the door to find a large group of laughing people there.

"Shower!" they called. "Happy shower!"

They entered with an ironing board, gifts, food, even plates and cups.

I watched, floored. What was happening? Shower? Was it raining? And what were these people from church, these people we barely knew, doing at our house at nine at night with all these things?

"For you, Marianne and George," they said. "To help fill your new house."

We had never heard of such a thing as a "shower," but it was just one more evidence of the continuing love and practical help faithfully given us by American believers. Bacsi even held a Bible study in our own modest home and brought along all his friends to participate with us. And each Sunday we were picked up for services.

Finally we received word that Australia had agreed to accept our visa application. It didn't seem possible after so much time and effort, but the end was finally in sight. I sighed with relief and prayed with renewed vigor.

Granny and Bacsi asked all their Christian friends to pray for us. I appreciated everyone's concern, and I was confident Australia would have our visas for us in no time.

Instead Australia did nothing, and I found out that I was pregnant again.

I had never been very good at planning pregnancies, but the timing of this one was disastrous. We had no home, no means of support, no country.

"When's the baby due?" George tried to pretend he wasn't upset.

"May."

He ran his hand through his hair. "Who knows where we'll be then!"

We were well aware that we could do nothing about the situation, that God was in control, but it was hard to get to the point where we could thank God for another unexpected circumstance.

The end of October arrived, our visa extension ran out, and there was still no word from Australia. We reported to Immigration and were told that there would be no new extension on our Visitor's Visas. We would be deported through government channels.

We felt like criminals. We were photographed, finger printed, and told to report to the immigration office regularly.

George and I were thoroughly depressed. We had prayed faithfully, were still praying. Many Christians were praying, even people we didn't know, and nothing seemed to be happening.

Weeks passed as we waited in turmoil. Ironically, the United States through diplomatic channels could do no better at finding us a home than we could. No one wanted us.

Now that George was no longer hampered by the regulations of his Visitor's Visa, he was able to find work. Bacsi helped him get a job as a cost study man on a construction job at Lynwood Gardens in Elkins Park in Northeast Philadelphia. It was good for him to have a specific job to do, a place to go every day.

At the end of February, one year after we left Europe,

our Australian visas and landing permit came through. We quickly began the process of trying to get boat or plane reservations for the four of us, but none were available. Tickets had to be bought months in advance, and as March passed and April arrived, we were no closer to leaving.

"Dr. Luders, it's such a mess!" I told my obstetrician during one of my weekly visits. "Australia has said they'll accept us, but we can't get tickets to get there. And when we do go, I won't know anyone, let alone any good doctors. And Immigration is upset with us — like we're holding up the tickets on purpose." I bit my lip. No tears, I told myself. "And I don't want to leave my American friends!"

"You mean you're thinking of traveling to Australia before the baby's born?" Dr. Luders was appalled. "In your condition? You're due in four or five weeks. I couldn't let you travel such a distance and guarantee your health, to say nothing of the baby's. No. A trip to Australia is out of the question."

"My doctor says I can't go now even if the tickets come through," I told the Immigration official on our next visit. "It wouldn't be safe."

"Why not?" he asked.

I looked at him in surprise. "I'm eight months pregnant."

"You'll have to bring a letter from your physician confirming that fact," he said as he stared at my extremely rounded figure.

The very next day I brought him a letter signed by Dr. Luders confirming my pregnancy. We were granted permission to stay in the United States until the baby was old enough to travel.

It was a great relief to George and me to know that the baby could be born under safe and known medical conditions with our friends near to help. We would still go to Australia, only two or three months later than planned.

On Saturday, May 20, 1950, as I was cleaning windows, I began my labor. The delivery was so quick and uneventful that I didn't have time to worry about language problems and the difficulties I might have letting the nurses know what I needed. Robert was born that night in Germantown Hospital, a healthy baby and a natural born American citizen.

Robert's citizenship was a complete surprise to us.

"You know, as a citizen, Robert has certain rights," Bacsi told us.

I looked at the little scrap of George and me in my arms. "This little one?"

Bacsi nodded. "Legally he cannot be deported."

"But the rest of us — Mari, John, Andrea, and me — we are about to be deported. Surely they don't break up families!" George was appalled at the idea.

"Not at all," Bacsi assured us. "What you do is file a petition in Robert's name with the congressman from this district requesting that Robert's parents be allowed to remain in this country permanently to support the new, little citizen.

"We can do this?" We were astounded.

We stared in amazement at our son, God's solution to our whole dilemma. Once again we saw His hand at work in spite of our ignorance and distress.

A formal petition was filed on Robert's behalf with Congressman Hugh Scott in May 1950. In a special act of Congress, the parents of Robert William Fischer were granted permission to remain in the United States in order to support said citizen.

Four years later, on Flag Day, June 14, 1954, George and I became proud citizens. We had studied the required United States history and the facts about how the

American government functions, and we passed a test given to us concerning this information.

As we stood in the courthouse that day to pledge allegiance to our new flag for the first time, I did not regret giving up my loyalty to Hungary. In all our years in America, I had never really missed my homeland. I'd missed the people certainly, especially my family, but I never regretted God's bringing us to this great land and working so many miracles to keep us here.

19

Mama

Mama was coming!

It had been seven years since that November morning we bid farewell to her and Papa in the Budapest train station, and we itched with the excitement of seeing her again. She had been allowed to leave Hungary permanently because of her age and the State's fallacious assumption that she was an expendable person.

We stood on the dock in New York City scanning the rails of the liner, looking for her. John and Andrea, nine and seven, kept telling Robert, five, how much he would love his grandmother. George and I looked at each other and grinned, knowing that most of the older children's memories of Mama were ones we had created for them.

Suddenly Mama was there, looking just the same, our Dumpling. What a joy to embrace her, to welcome her to our adopted country.

When I examined my feelings at Mama's coming, I found them a curious mixture of joy tinged with sorrow. For Mama had come to us alone; Papa would never join her in our new home in Willow Grove, north of Philadelphia.

When the telegram had come two years ago informing us of Papa's death, I had been crushed. I had not accepted the idea that I would never see him again. I had always assumed — against reason — that we would be re-united.

If I had known, that long ago day when he had laid his head on my shoulder and wept, that I would never see him again, I wondered if I would have had the strength to leave him.

As I grieved for Papa, a letter arrived from Klara, my cousin and now a sister in the Messiah. She told me of her visit with Papa in the hospital. There she shared again the claims of Jesus Christ with him, and he accepted Jesus as his Messiah as she prayed with him. My heart sang at the thought of seeing Papa again in the Lord's presence.

Of difficulty for Mama — besides Papa's absence — was that to join her daughter in America, she had to leave her sons and their families in Hungary. It was our constant concern that neither Alex nor Jules was inclined to accept the Party line, and we knew only too well the fate that awaited those who dissented.

Still, as we drove home from New York with Mama in the back seat of our car, the children climbing all over her before falling asleep on her ample bosom, my heart was warmed. God was good.

In the years since we'd left the chef's home and moved into the tiny row house, George had worked at Cottman Builders Supply. He was now a manager at the concrete block plant, and in 1951 he had been able to buy his first car. Now we could take ourselves to church and the store, and George could drive himself to work.

In 1952 I learned to drive. It was a strange feeling to have so much power at my control, and the first times I drove alone, my knees shook and my heart thudded.

For some time I had been visiting the developments being built in the Philadelphia suburbs, looking at houses, praying for one of our own.

One Sunday afternoon when we visited a sample house, George began talking with its builder, a man he knew from Cottman's. We liked this house, especially its large kitchen. The builder and George reached an agreement that if we paid a minimum downpayment of $200 plus settlement, the builder would underwrite the mortgage.

We took this man's help as a sign from the Lord and with great joy purchased our first home in spring, 1955.

It was about this time that we received word of my old friend Peter Schuck. Peter had issued himself a passport and defected to Sweden. Somehow the news did not surprise me. Peter always survived with catlike grace. I remembered him with affection as a young boy swimming in the Hungarian summer sun, as a young man who endured the horrors of war and still smiled, as an official who assisted us in our escape to freedom. Ever jaunty and always indomitable, Peter settled in Stockholm where he lived until his death years later.

The ease with which Mama fit into our lives pleased me. She seemed to enjoy this country though she never did master the language. Instead she spoke with her smile and loving gestures. Soon everyone loved her as we did.

It was a delight to share my home with Mama, and she loved caring for her grandchildren. Because of Mama's helpful presence, I found I had some free time. I began to think of photography. I have an instinctive urge to create photos, and perhaps I could now satisfy that desire.

I found William Feinstein, an established photographer who needed an assistant. It was a pleasure to work for him, a joy to be back at the retouching table.

It wasn't long after I began working that I discovered that I was pregnant again. Though the pregnancy was unplanned, we awaited the baby's arrival with great anticipation.

Fall, 1956, also brought another event of great import

to us. In Hungary, there was a temporary break in the Iron Curtain. The Magyars rebelled against the depth of the Russian involvement in their country and struggled to become an independent nation again.

We followed the news of the Hungarian Revolution with great hope. Not since World War II had we been so anxious, so concerned. We watched the TV, listened to the radio, and read the newspapers. We hoped against hope that the United States would intervene on behalf of the revolutionaries, but the Suez Canal Crisis arose, shifting the attention of the State Department from our homeland.

Sadly it was only a matter of days that Hungary tasted the heady wine of autonomy. Then the Russian tanks moved in, and the Curtain slammed down more snugly than ever.

What effect had the short-lived Revolution had on Alex and Jules and their families? We knew Jules had already served two years of an eight-year prison sentence on false charges of political dissent. One of the years of his sentence was for the crime of having a sister who was an American citizen.

Surely both he and Alex had been involved in the uprising somehow. Were they all right? Had they been injured? Killed? Punished?

The timing of my pregnancy was again a godsend. As I neared my late November due date, Mama was kept busy caring for me and the children. When Sylvia was born on November 27, 1956, Mama had even less time to fret over her sons and the curious lack of news from them.

Christmas came, and the New Year. Then on January 12, 1957, the phone rang.

"Hello," I said.

"Mari, it's Jules."

"Jules!" I was momentarily paralyzed with the wonderful shock of hearing his voice. Then, "Mama, I'm talking to Jules!"

We talked and cried and thanked God for his safety. He was calling from Vienna where he and Cornelia and four-year-old Sylvia as well as Alex and Agnes and six-year-old Tommy and three-year-old Gabriella were staying.

"Come to America," we urged. "We will sponsor you. The immigration quotas have been set aside for any Hungarian with relatives in the United States. Come!"

They came. In late April we went to Camp Kilmer, New Jersey, to meet Jules and Cornelia and Sylvia. In late May we drove to Brooklyn to meet Alex and Agnes and the children.

Mama was overjoyed. Her family was complete again, all safe and secure. She — and we — listened amazed as my brothers and their families, seated in my living room, told the saga of their escape.

"During the Revolution," said Jules, "the prisons were opened and all political prisoners were freed. When it became apparent that the Revolution was doomed, we knew we'd have to leave the country. We tried to escape once, only to be apprehended at the border. When they took us back to Budapest, they called us 'voluntary returnees,' and we weren't punished."

"But as soon as possible, we tried again," said Alex. "Our building superintendent had some connections, and for a goodly sum of money, he directed us to a section of the border where the soldiers were known to look the other way if it was worth their while."

"We went by bus as far as we could," said Jules. "Then we began walking across some fairly open farmland toward the border. I was carrying Sylvia, and Alex had Gabriella whom we'd drugged so she wouldn't cry out."

"Then some soldiers spotted us and began to shoot,"

said Cornelia. "I was sure we would either be captured or killed. I was so afraid for the children!"

Agnes nodded. "Tommy and I gripped hands so tightly it pained as we ran through the fields and finally hid in the stubble left from the harvest. After a time the soldiers stopped shooting and disappeared. We hurried on through some trees until suddenly we saw a lady. She was an Austrian! We were free! She kept us for the night and helped us get off for Vienna the next day."

It was amazing to me as I looked around my living room. My whole family was here! And George's entire family was also out of Hungary. One at a time over the years his brothers and sisters and Mother and Father had come to North America until only Leslie had remained behind. In the turmoil following the Revolution, he and Maca and their son had escaped in much the same fashion as Alex and Jules. All were free.

The only thing that marred my world was Mama's inability to accept the claims of my Messiah. In the years she had been with us, she had come to the weekly Bible study we had in our home where she listened attentively as I translated for her. She went to church with us sometimes, and she never seemed distressed at what we believed. One vacation at a Bible conference, she even sat in the meeting and listened to my translation.

But whenever I questioned her about the Messiah, her answer was always the same. She could not let go of her traditions, but more importantly, she couldn't understand why Christ should die for her.

One day as I prayed about Mama, a word filtered through my mind over and over again. Believe. Believe. Believe.

But, Lord, I do believe.

"Believe on the Lord Jesus Christ and thou shalt be saved."

Suddenly I realized that this was the answer for Mama. Only believe. Not change. Not fully understand. Not give up her traditions. Just believe.

I approached Mama again.

"Mama, you don't have to give up your traditions or who you are to accept the Messiah. You only have to believe that Jesus died in your place and for your sins — the perfect atonment. Listen. 'For God so loved the world, that He gave his only begotten Son, that whosoever believeth in Him should not perish, but have everlasting life.' Do you believe that, Mama?"

Mama said nothing, so I tried again.

"Mama, can you put your name in that verse and believe that God gave his Son for you? 'For God so loved Erzsebet Komlos that He gave His only begotten Son that if Erzsebet Komlos believeth in him, Erzsebet Komlos shall not perish but have everlasting life.' "

Mama thought for a moment. Then, "This I can do."

Tears filled our eyes as we looked at each other. At 79, Mama had become a child of God. A year later she entered into the Messiah's presence.

I marvel as I look back over my life and see God's hand at work. That night in the airraid shelter when He told me, "Because thou hast made the Lord, which is my refuge, even the most High, thy habitation; there shall no evil befall thee, neither shall any plague come nigh thy dwelling. For He shall give His angels charge over thee . . ." I had no idea of the extent of the miracles He would work for us.

What a Messiah He has proved to be!

CHRISTIAN HERALD ASSOCIATION AND ITS MINISTRIES

CHRISTIAN HERALD ASSOCIATION, founded in 1878, publishes The Christian Herald Magazine, one of the leading interdenominational religious monthlies in America. Through its wide circulation, it brings inspiring articles and the latest news of religious developments to many families. From the magazine's pages came the initiative for CHRISTIAN HERALD CHILDREN'S HOME and THE BOWERY MISSION, two individually supported not-for-profit corporations.

CHRISTIAN HERALD CHILDREN'S HOME, established in 1894, is the name for a unique and dynamic ministry to disadvantaged children, offering hope and opportunities which would not otherwise be available for reasons of poverty and neglect. The goal is to develop each child's potential and to demonstrate Christian compassion and understanding to children in need.

Mont Lawn is a permanent camp located in Bushkill, Pennsylvania. It is the focal point of a ministry which provides a healthful "vacation with a purpose" to children who without it would be confined to the streets of the city. Up to 1000 children between the ages of 7 and 11 come to Mont Lawn each year.

Christian Herald Children's Home maintains year-round contact with children by means of an *In-City Youth Ministry.* Central to its philosophy is the belief that only through sustained relationships and demonstrated concern can individual lives be truly enriched. Special emphasis is on individual guidance, spiritual and family counseling and tutoring. This follow-up ministry to inner-city children culminates for many in financial assistance toward higher education and career counseling.

THE BOWERY MISSION, located at 227 Bowery, New York City, has since 1879 been reaching out to the lost men on the Bowery, offering them what could be their last chance to rebuild their lives. Every man is fed, clothed and ministered to. Countless numbers have entered the 90-day residential rehabilitation program at the Bowery Mission. A concentrated ministry of counseling, medical care, nutrition therapy, Bible study and Gospel services awakens a man to spiritual renewal within himself.

These ministries are supported solely by the voluntary contributions of individuals and by legacies and bequests. Contributions are tax deductible. Checks should be made out either to CHRISTIAN HERALD CHILDREN'S HOME or to THE BOWERY MISSION.

Administrative Office: 40 Overlook Drive, Chappaqua, New York 10514
Telephone: (914) 769-9000